Nineteenth-Century American Choral Music

Fallen Leaf Reference Books in Music, ISSN 8755-268X

Nineteenth-Century American Choral Music:

An Annotated Guide

by David P. DeVenney

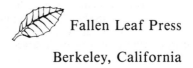 Fallen Leaf Press

Berkeley, California

Published by Fallen Leaf Press
P.O. Box 10034
Berkeley, California 94709

Printed in the United States of America

Library of Congress Cataloging-in-Publication Data

DeVenney, David P., 1958–
Nineteenth-Century American Choral Music.
(Fallen Leaf reference books in music,
ISSN 8755-286X; no. 8)
Bibliography: p. Includes indexes.
1. Choruses—19th century—Bibliography. 2. Choral music—
United States—19th century—Bibliography. I. Title. II.
Series.
    ML128 C48D48 1987   016.7841'00973   87-80918
            ISBN 0-914913-08-5 (pbk.)

to my parents

TABLE OF CONTENTS

viii

TABLE OF CONTENTS

PREFACE

The choral music of early American composers, particularly that of William Billings, is relatively well-known to American conductors and scholars. The same may be said about choral music of the twentieth century. The music of the nineteenth century, however, has long been neglected. My primary aim in writing this book has been to provide the bibliographic groundwork for the study and performance of these compositions.

A wealth of choral music was written and performed during the nineteenth century in the United States. I have included nearly thirteen hundred compositions in this volume, limited (as explained in the Guide to Use) to those written for "legitimate" choral ensembles. The works range in style from the early, nationalistic music of Anthony Philip Heinrich, to the experimental, more daring pieces of Charles Ives, which foreshadowed later music of the twentieth century.

These choral works were written for a large variety of occasions. Many of the composers supported themselves by directing church choirs or community choral groups. Naturally, they wrote music to supply these ensembles with literature to sing. Such groups as the Boston Handel and Haydn Society were influential not only in commissioning new choral works, but in setting standards of repertory and performance that other

x Preface

groups imitated. Men's choruses, women's choruses, and organizations such as the Apollo Club of Boston and the Mendelssohn
Club of Philadelphia also commissioned new choral music.

Paine, Edward MacDowell, and Horatio Parker wrote music
for such functions as commencement and the installation of a
new president at the universities where they taught. Mac-
Dowell, at Columbia University, also left a number of college
fight songs. Finally, many of the choral works listed here
were written for the large number of music festivals that dot-
ted the Eastern United States.

The earliest composer listed here is Anthony Philip
Heinrich. His music is simple and straightforward, in part
because he began writing music as an untutored composer. His
straightforward style also reflected his response to the nat-
ural grandeur of the new nation and its unspoiled wilderness,
which deeply moved him.

Heinrich, called the "Beethoven of America" by contemporary critics, studied music in London in 1827 and returned
to America in 1832 to resume his career as a composer. His
oratorios, symphonies, and other large-scale works bear such
titles as The Dawning of Music in Kentucky; or, the Pleasures
of Harmony in the Solitudes of Nature, and The Western Minstrel. Heinrich's works are extremely nationalistic; his
choral music is no exception.

William Henry Fry, a contemporary of Heinrich's, was also
a nationalistic composer. He is perhaps best known for his
opera Leonora (1845), the first publicly performed American
"grand" opera in the United States. He was trained as a musician and his works are consequently more learned in style and
technique than Heinrich's.

It was the "father" of music education in America, Lowell

Mason, who moved choral composition and performance away from the "singing school" traditions of early choral music in this country to a technical level meeting European standards. While he made his largest contribution to choral music by introducing the works of European composers to American school children, church choirs, and concert audiences, Mason also wrote a vast number of songs, school choruses, and hymns, as well as a number of anthems and partsongs. The latter are included here.

John Knowles Paine was perhaps the most important and influential voice in music in this country during the nineteenth century. In 1839, Paine was born into a musical family in Portland, Maine, where he received his early training. He completed his musical education in Germany, where increasing numbers of young American composers went to perfect their craft.

On his return to the United States in 1861, Paine was appointed instructor of music at Harvard College and later became the first professor of music there in 1875. It was from this position that he was most influential: his students included Arthur Foote, John Alden Carpenter, Daniel Gregory Mason, Archibald T. Davison, and a great many other leading American musicians.

Paine's major choral works include The Nativity and The Realm of Fancy, for soli, mixed chorus, and orchestra, and Phoebus Arise, for men's chorus and orchestra. His St. Peter was favorably compared by a contemporary critic to Mendelssohn's Elijah. St. Peter was perhaps contemporary audiences' favorite work by Paine, although the composition that reflects most favorably upon him from the prospect of the twentieth century is the Mass in D. The Mass is a powerful, classically conceived work in which one hears echoes of Brahms and Men-

delssohn. It is a work that deserves to re-enter the repertory of modern choral ensembles and oratorio societies.

With Paine in Boston was a group of composers -- George
Chadwick, Arthur Foote, Horatio Parker, Arthur Whiting, and
Amy Marcy Cheney Beach -- considered his heirs and known as
the Boston Classicists. With the exception of Foote, all of
these musicians studied in Europe and, though their styles
differ widely, their music shares the use of classical forms,
regularity of phrase structure, and academically correct harmonies and counterpoint.

Chadwick is best remembered for his operas and his pro-
grammatic symphonies. His many choral works include anthems
and partsongs. His Symphonic Sketches, a musical suite, contains two movements, "Jubilee" and "Nöel," that are set for
chorus and orchestra. Phoenix expirans for soli, mixed
chorus, and orchestra is also an important work.

The catalog of the works of Arthur Foote is one of the
longest in this volume. Foote left 112 choral works in vir-
tually every genre, sacred and secular: partsongs, anthems,
service music, and major works with orchestra. His most well-
known work is The Wreck of the Hesperus, a full-blown Romantic
setting of a text by Henry W. Longfellow.

Amy Marcy Cheney (Mrs. H. H. A.) Beach is the only woman
composer included in this study. Like Foote, she left many
works in a variety of styles and genres. Several of her longer works, The Chambered Nautilus, The Rose of Avontown, and
The Sea Fairies, were written for women's voices. The choral
work for which she is most remembered is the Mass in E-flat,
which, like Paine's Mass in D Minor, is a rich work that deserves to be performed today.

Arguably the most important American choral work of the

entire nineteenth century, and a work that still   receives oc-
casional   performances,   is   Horatio   Parker's   Hora novissima.
Considered to be his masterpiece, the oratorio is divided into
two parts and contains eleven numbers; each half closes with a
grand chorus for the full   ensemble.   Parker   was   clearly a
master of classical, European musical technique.   This is seen
most clearly in the double-chorus "There stand those   halls on
high":   the   use   of   hemiola   and   cross-rhythms drives the
movement forward to a climactic conclusion,   where both choirs
join together in a majestic twelve-eight section.

     Several   other   composers   should   be   mentioned briefly.
James Cutler Dunn Parker contributed most   through   his religious service music: he wrote nine settings of the Te Deum
alone.   Henry Kimball Hadley (a pupil of Chadwick) was   a prolific composer   at his   best in   the secular cantatas, such as
The Admiral of the Seas.   Although   Charles   Martin Loeffler
wrote only   a few   choral works,   these show great imagination
and use of color.   Loeffler   wrote for   such "exotic" instru-
ments as   the viola d'amore and   viola da gamba, and for such
combinations as cello, two   flutes, harp,   and organ.   Edward
MacDowell   was   both   prolific   and influential and his choral
works, including a number   for men's   voices, are   some of the
finest of the period.   He was the foremost craftsman of smaller forms like the partsong.

     Finally, we come to Charles Ives, who left a wide variety
of choral   works.   Some, such as He is There!, are quite conservative in style and   approach.   Others, such   as Psalm 90,
with its   rhythmic complexities, and Psalm 67, with its use of
two tonal centers, paved new roads for later composers to follow.   Although his techniques are undoubtedly of the twentieth
century, his motivation was Romantic, and thus I have included

him here.

Although some of the lesser choral works of nineteenth-
century America no longer appeal to us because of their trite
harmonies and clichéd melodic materials, the compositions men-
tioned above, and dozens more described in these pages, are
among the very best works that have been penned by American
composers. They will happily bear close examination and study
and, more importantly, they deserve our attention as performers and listeners.

* * *

One cannot complete a project of this sort without the
help and cooperation of a great many libraries and their
staffs. In particular, I would like to thank Richard Jackson
and the staff of the New York Public Library for their assis-
tance in answering many questions as I was just beginning my
research. I also extend my thanks to the staff of the Harvard
University Libraries (especially Holly E. Mockovak of the music library, who went out of her way to be helpful) and Brenda
Wilson of the Courtwright Memorial Library at Otterbein College, as well as the staffs of the music libraries of The Ohio
State University and the College-Conservatory of Music, University of Cincinnati.

The following institutions and people were kind enough to
help through correspondence: the American Academy and Institute of Arts and Letters, American University School of Music, Chicago Historical Society, Chicago Public Library, Columbia University Music Library, Connecticut Historical Soci-

ety, Free Library of Philadelphia, Isabella Stewart Gardner
Museum, Hartford (Connecticut) Public Library, Historical
Society of Pennsylvania, Hope Publishing Company, Walter S.
Jenkins, the Library Company of Philadelphia, Library of Con-
gress, New England Conservatory of Music, Peterborough (New
Hampshire) Town Library, Washington State University Music
Library, Westminster Choir College, and the Yale University
Music Library.

My colleagues at Otterbein College have been most sup-
portive, in particular Dr. Donald C. Bulthaup, Vice-President
for Academic Affairs, through whose generosity I received
travel funding to consult library holdings; Dr. Morton Achter,
the chairman of the Department of Music; and Mr. Craig
Johnson, my choral music colleague and friend.   Finally, I
must thank my close friend David DeCooman, whose support and
patience helped make this book possible.

GUIDE TO USE

The Catalog of Works

The Catalog of Works lists choral music by composers who were active in the United States during the nineteenth century and died or ceased composing after the end of the First World War (ca. 1920). Only those composers who wrote serious, "art" music are included. Composers such as Stephen Foster, though important to the history of nineteenth-century American music, are not included because they are primarily considered popular composers.

The Catalog of Works is arranged alphabetically by composer, subarranged alphabetically by titles of works. Each work is provided with a four-digit reference number; these numbers run consecutively throughout the first section and are used in all of the compositional indexes to refer the reader to a specific composition.

For works that contain a number of compositions (such as MacDowell's Drei Lieder für vierstimmigen Männerchor, which consists of three separate compositions), the complete annotation appears only under the main heading (Drei Lieder, etc.). Each of the compositions within that heading has its own reference number but refers the reader to the main heading for a complete annotation.

Each work is followed by an annotation that gives an opus number for the work and the date of composition, as well as performing forces, the author of the text, the duration of the

work (if over ten minutes), the published editions of the work
(giving both publisher and publication year), and, if possible, the location of the manuscript. Durations are given only
for the longer choral works for two reasons. First, I felt
that a work shorter than ten minutes could easily be included
in a choral program; the vast majority of anthems and partsongs by these composers fall into this category, and to time
each of these short works did not seem feasible or even worth-
while. Secondly, a work of ten minutes or more would take up
a significant part of a program and hence it would be important for a director to be aware of its duration. Timings of
these works are based on careful examinations of the scores,
but should be taken merely as a guide.

The last item of each annotation is a cross-reference to
articles in the Bibliography that deal with that specific
work. Articles of a more general nature are not cross-refer-
enced in the Catalog but will be found under the appropriate
headings in the Bibliography.

I have listed a number of works for which I have little
or no information other than the title. I included these
titles if they were also included in an authoritative biography or list of works by another author.

The majority of the works listed are original compositions intended to be sung by a choral ensemble as opposed to
compositions written for an ensemble of solo voices. Dudley
Buck's works written for "Quartet or chorus," for example,
are not included for this reason; they were originally
intended to be sung by solo voices (the New York Public
Library classifies them as "songs").

Also included are a composer's arrangements for choir of
his or her own works. If the original was a song, the choral

arrangement is treated as an original composition. If the
original work was for chorus, the original voicing is given.
For example, an arrangement of a work for male chorus would
follow the listing of the same work for mixed voices if the
original composition was for SATB choir. In this case, the
annotation following the listing for male voices would refer
the reader back to the annotation for the original SATB composition.

Included are original compositions intended to be sung by
a choral ensemble as well as choral arrangements by these composers of their own works. Excluded are these composers'
hymns, hymn tunes, melodies borrowed from folk tunes, and arrangements of other composers' works. Also excluded are works
written for the stage; individual choruses taken from stage
works; choruses published separately from larger works; didac-
tic choruses for use in schools or churches (such as Lowell
Mason's Song Garden); and songs in which the refrain has an
optional choral ending (such as George Root's "The Vacant
Chair," called "a song and a chorus").

The Bibliography

The second section of the book is an annotated bibliography of writings on nineteenth-century American choral
music. The bibliography contains information on the history
and circumstances surrounding the composition of these works
as well as theoretical and analytical studies. In addition,
it contains writings on the performance practice and inter-
pretation of these composers' choral music. This bibliography

was primarily conceived as a research tool for the choral conductor who wishes to have a comprehensive list of writings specifically concerned with nineteenth-century American choral music, as well as the conductor who would like to explore this literature in more depth.

The bibliography treats only those writings directly concerning nineteenth-century American choral music. Books such as Barbara Zuck's <u>A History of Musical Americanism</u> (Ann Arbor: UMI Research Press, 1980) are not included because they do not pertain directly to these works. When possible, however, I searched the bibliographies and footnotes of books such as Zuck's for sources of other, more specific writings.

The citations are arranged alphabetically by author. Each citation is preceded by a three-digit reference number. These numbers are independent from those used in the first section of the book and are used only in the indexes relevant to the bibliography.

Complete bibliographical data have been supplied whenever possible for each entry. Sometimes, however, the source of the article did not have a complete citation and I was unable to locate the document for study. I decided it was best to include the incomplete citation rather than exclude the article.

Whenever I was able to obtain a document I indicated this in bibliographic citation. When I was not able to obtain the document, I took the annotation from another source if possible (<u>RILM</u> or <u>Dissertation Abstracts</u>, for example).

The bibliography includes European and American doctoral dissertations and masters' theses, as well as articles in Festschriften and other collected papers, articles in scholarly journals, and books. Memoirs and collected recollections

of these composers are included when appropriate, as are their
letters and reviews of performances of their works.

Excluded are program notes, reviews of recordings, thematic catalogs, and iconographies except where these are con-
tained in another, non-specialized source. Articles in dic-
tionaries and encyclopedias are also excluded, but whenever
possible I have consulted the bibliographies of these volumes
for additional sources.

The Indexes

This volume contains ten indexes separated into two parts
dealing with the respective parts of this study, the catalog
of works and the bibliography. The choral works themselves
are indexed by genre, by title, and by the author of the text,
although only for those texts that are non-biblical and non-
liturgical, since these types of texts are commonly set to
music and are relatively easy to locate. The bibliography has
a separate index. For a complete listing, please refer to the
Table of Contents.

Finally the Appendix to the book contains a listing of
the music publishers cited in the Catalog of Works in the
annotations following each choral work listed.

Guide to Annotations in Catalog of Works

0000   Title, Opus number, Date of Composition
   2.   Performing Forces Required
   3.   Author and/or Translator of Text
   4.   Duration (if over ten minutes)
   5.   Publisher and Date(s) of Publication
   6.   Location of Manuscript
   7.   Relevant citations from the Bibliography of
        Writings

Library abbreviations:
   Harvard   Harvard University Libraries; Cambridge,
                           Massachusetts
   L of C   Library Of Congress; Washington, D.C.
   New England Cons.   New England Conservatory of Music
                           Boston, Massachusetts
   Yale   Yale University Libraries; New Haven,
                           Connecticut

All other libraries cited are given a complete name and
location.

CATALOG OF WORKS

CATALOG OF WORKS

B E A C H

0001 Agnus Dei
2. SATB, organ
3. liturgical
5. Schmidt, 1936

0002 Ah, Love, But a Day!,
Op. 44, No.2
2. SSAA, piano
3. Robert Browning
5. Schmidt, 1927

0003 All Hail the Power, Op.
74, 1915
2. SATB, organ
3. Edward Perronet
5. G. Schirmer, 1915

**0004 Alleluia! Christ is
Risen**, Op. 27, 1895
2. SATB
5. Schmidt

0005 Around the Manger, Op.
115, 1925?
2. SATB, organ or piano
3. Robert Davis
5. Ditson, 1925

0006 same for SSAA
5. Ditson, 1929
6. L of C

**0007 Benedicite, omnis
opera: see Service in A,**
Op. 121.

**0008 Benedictus: see
Service in A, Op. 121.**

**0009 Benedictus es Domine
and Benedictus, Op. 103,**
1924?
2. SATB
3. liturgical
5. Ditson, 1924

0010 Bethlehem, Op. 24,
1893
2. SATB, organ
5. Schmidt, 1893

**0011 The Bluebell: see
Three Flower Songs.**

0012 Bonum est, confiteri,
Op. 76, No. 1
2. S solo, SATB, organ
3. biblical
5. G. Schirmer, 1916

0013 The Candy Lion, Op.
75, No. 1, 1915
2. SSAA, piano

BEACH

3. Abbie Farewell Brown
5. G. Schirmer, 1915

0014 The Canticle of the
Sun, Op. 123, 1925
2. SATB soli, SATB,
orchestra
3. St. Francis of Assisi,
trans. Matthew Arnold
4. 21 minutes
5. Schmidt, 1928
6. New England Cons.

0015 The Chambered Nautilus,
Op. 66, 1907
2. SA soli, SSAA, orchestra
3. Oliver Wendell Holmes
4. 18 minutes
5. Schmidt, 1907
6. New England Cons.
(holograph orchestral
version); University of
Missouri-Kansas City
(autograph); L of C
(autograph)

0016 Christ in the Universe,
Op. 139 (132?), 1931
2. AT soli, SATB, orchestra
3. Alice Meynell
4. 21 minutes
5. H.W. Gray, 1931
7. 120

0017 Christmas Anthem: see
Peace on Earth.

0018 The Clover: see Three
Flower Songs.

0019 Come Unto These Yellow
Sands, Op. 39, No. 2
2. SSAA

3. Shakespeare
5. Schmidt, 1897
6. L of C

0020 Communion Responses:
see Service in A, Op. 121.

0021 Communion Service and
Lamb of God, Op. 122, 1928
2. SATB
5. Schmidt

0022 Constant Christmas,
Op. 95, 1922
2. SA soli, SATB, organ
5. Presser, 1922

0023 Dolladine, Op. 75, No.
3, 1915
2. SSAA
3. William Brightly Hands
5. G. Schirmer, 1915

0024 Drowsy Dreamtown, Op.
129, 1932
2. S solo, SSA, piano
3. Robert Norwood
5. Schmidt, 1932

0025 Dusk in June, Op. 82,
1917
2. SSAA, piano ad lib.
3. Sara Teasdale
5. G. Schirmer, 1917

0026 Easter Anthem: Christ
is Risen: see Alleluia!
Christ is Risen.

0027 Evening Hymn, Op. 125,
No. 2
2. S solo, SATB, piano

BEACH

3. Adelaide A. Procter
5. Schmidt, 1936

0028 Fairy Lullaby, Op. 37,
   No. 3
2. SSAA, piano
3. Shakespeare
5. Schmidt, 1907

0029 Far Awa'!, Op. 43, No.
   4
2. SSA, piano
3. Robert Burns
5. Schmidt, 1918

0030 Festival Jubilate, Op.
   17, 1892
2. SSAATTB, orchestra
3. biblical
4. 15 minutes
5. Schmidt, 1892
6. New England Cons.

0031 Four Canticles, Op. 78,
   1916
2. SATB
5. G. Schirmer

0032 Four Choral Responses,
   1932?
2. SATB
5. J. Fischer

0033 The Greenwood, Op. 110,
   1925
2. SATB
3. William Lisle (Lyle)
   Bowles
5. C.C. Birchard, 1925

0034 Hearken Unto Me, Op.
   139, 1934 (1933?)
2. SATB soli, SATB, organ
3. biblical
4. 14 minutes
5. Schmidt, 1934

0035 Help Us, O God, Op.
   50, 1903
2. SATB
3. biblical
4. 12 minutes
5. Schmidt, 1903
6. L of C

0036 A Hymn of Freedom,
   Op. 52, 1903
2. SATB, organ
3. Samuel F. Smith
5. Schmidt, 1903
6. L of C; Boston Public
   Lib. (facsimile)
N.B.: also published with
the text "O Lord Our God
Arise," 1924.

0037 Hymn of Trust, Op. 13
2. SATB
3. Oliver Wendell Holmes
5. Schmidt, 1901

0038 I Will Give Thanks,
   Op. 147, 1939
2. S solo, SATB, organ
3. biblical
6. Washington State Univ.

0039 I Will Lift Up Mine
   Eyes, Op. 98, 1923
2. SATB
3. biblical
5. Presser, 1923

BEACH

0040 An Indian Lullaby
2. SSAA
5. The World's Best Music,
    ed. Johnson and Dean.
    N.Y.: 1899. Vol. I, p.
    169-73.

**0041 Jubilate: see Service
    in A**, Op. 121.

0042 June, Op. 51, No. 3
2. SSAA, piano
3. Erich Jansen
5. Schmidt, 1917

0043 same for SATB
5. Schmidt, 1931

0044 The Last Prayer, Op.
    126, No. 1, 1931
2. TTBB
5. Schmidt

**0045 Let This Mind Be in
    You**, Op. 105, 1924
2. SB soli, SATB, organ
3. biblical paraphrase
5. Church, 1924

0046 The Little Brown Bee,
    Op. 8 (9?), 1891
2. SSAA
3. Margaret Eytinge
5. Schmidt, 1891
6. L of C

**0047 The Lord is My
    Shepherd**, Op. 96, 1923
2. SSA, organ
3. biblical

4. 11 minutes
5. Presser, 1923

0048 Lord of All Beings,
    Op. 146, 1937
2. SATB
5. H.W. Gray

**0049 Lord of the Worlds
    Above**, Op. 109, 1925?
2. SB soli, SATB, organ
5. Ditson, 1925

**0050 Magnificat: see
    Service in A**, Op. 121.

0051 Mass in E-flat, Op. 5,
    1890
2. SATB soli, SATB,
    orchestra
3. liturgical
4. 35 minutes
5. Schmidt, 1890, 1918
6. New England Cons. (or-
    chestral version); Univ.
    of Missouri-Kansas City
    (autograph of "Gradual")
7. 014, 070

0052 May Eve, Op. 86, 1933
2. SATB, piano
3. Thomas S. Jones, Jr.
5. A Book of Choruses,
    Silver Burdett, 1923

**0053 The Minstrel and the
    King**, Op. 16, 1894
2. TBar soli, TTBB,
    orchestra
3. Friedrich von Schiller
4. 22 minutes
5. Schmidt, 1894
6. New England Cons.
    (orchestral version); L
    of C (piano version)

BEACH

0054 The Moon Boat and Who
Has Seen the Wind, Op. 118,
1929-30?
2. SATB
5. Summy-Birchard, 1929,
1930

0055 Nunc dimittis: see
Responses.

0056 Nunc dimittis: see
Service in A, Op. 121.

0057 O Lord God of Israel,
Op. 141
2. SAB soli, SATB, organ
3. biblical
6. L of C (facsimile)

0058 O Lord Our God Arise:
see A Hymn of Freedom.

0059 O Praise the Lord, All
Ye Nations, Op. 7, 1891
2. SATB, organ
3. biblical
5. Schmidt, 1891

0060 One Morning Very Early,
Op. 144, 1937
2. SSA
5. Schmidt

0061 One Summer Day, Op. 57,
No. 2
2. SSAA
3. Agnes Lockhart
5. Schmidt, 1904
6. L of C

0062 Only a Song, Op. 57,
No. 1
2. SSAA
3. Agnes Lockhart
5. Schmidt, 1904
6. L of C

0063 Over Hill Over Dale,
Op. 39, No. 1
2. SSAA
3. Shakespeare
5. Schmidt, 1897
6. L of C

0064 Panama Hymn, Op. 74,
1915
2. SATB, organ or piano
3. Wendell Phillips
Stafford
5. G. Schirmer, 1915
N.B.: "All Hail the Power of
Jesus' Name" also bears the
marking Op. 74.

0065 Pax nobiscum, 1920
2. SSA, organ
3. Earl Marlatt
5. H.W. Gray, 1944

0066 Peace I Leave With
You: see Responses.

0067 Peace on Earth, Op.
38, 1897
2. SATB, organ
5. Schmidt, 1897
6. L of C

0068 Peter Pan, Op. 101,
1923
2. SSA, piano
3. Jessie Andrews
4. 12 minutes
5. Presser, 1923

BEACH

0069 Psalm 111: see I Will
Give Thanks.

0070 Responses, Op. 8, 1891
2. SATB, organ
3. liturgical
5. Schmidt, 1891
6. L of C (b and c only)
 a. Nunc dimittis
 b. Peace I Leave with
 You
 c. With Prayer and
 Supplication

0071 The Rose of Avontown,
Op. 30, 1896
2. S solo, SSAA, orchestra
3. Caroline Mischka
4. 11-12 minutes
5. Schmidt, 1896, 1901,
1924
6. New England Cons.

0072 The Sea Fairies, Op.
59, 1904
2. SA soli, SSAA, orchestra
3. Alfred Lord Tennyson
4. 18 minutes
5. Schmidt, 1904
5. New England Cons.
(orchestral version); L
of C (piano version)

0073 Sea Fever, Op. 126, No.
2, 1931
2. TTBB, piano
3. John Masefield
5. Schmidt, 1931

0074 Service in A, Op. 63a-
e; Op. 121; Op. 122; 1928
2. SATB soli, SATB, organ

3. biblical/liturgical
4. 30 minutes
5. Schmidt, 1905, 1928,
1932
6. L of C (Op. 63a-e)
 a. Te Deum
 b. Benedictus
 c. Jubilate Deo
 d. Magnificat
 e. Nunc dimittis
 f. Benedicite omnis
 opera
 g. Communion Responses

0075 Shena Van, Op. 56, No.
4
2. SATB, piano
3. William Black
5. Schmidt, 1919
6. L of C

0076 same for TTBB
5. Schmidt, 1917

0077 same for SSA
5. Schmidt, 1917

0078 Song of Liberty, Op.
49, 1902
2. SATB
5. Schmidt

0079 Song of Welcome, Op.
42, 1894
2. SATB, orchestra
3. Henry Blossom, Jr.
5. Schmidt, 1898

0080 Sylvania, Op. 46, 1901
2. SATB soli, SSAATTBB,
orchestra
3. Frederick W. Banckroft,
from Walter Blöm
4. 30 minutes

BEACH

5. Schmidt, 1901
6. New England Cons.
    (orchestral version); L
    of C (piano version)

**0081 Te Deum: see Service
in A, Op. 121**

**0082 Te Deum in F, Op. 84,
1921, 1922**
2. S or T solo, SATB; or T
    solo, TTBB
3. liturgical
5. Presser, 1922
6. Boston Public Lib. (both
    versions, as well as
    correspondence relating
    to compositions)
7. 018
N.B.: 1st version in D maj.
for TTBB, 1921.

**0083 This Morning Very
Early, Op. 144**
2. SSA, piano
3. Patricia Louise Hiles
5. Schmidt, 1937

**0084 Thou Knowest, Lord, Op.
76, No. 2, 1914**
2. TB soli, SATB, organ
3. Jane Borthwick
5. G. Schirmer, 1915

**0085 Three Flower Songs, Op.
31, 1896**
2. SSAA
3. Margaret Deland
5. Schmidt, 1896
6. L of C
    a. The Clover
    b. The Yellow Daisy
    c. The Bluebell

**0086 Three School Songs,
Op. 94, 1923**
2. SATB
5. Hines, Hayden and
    Eldridge

**0087 Three Shakespeare
Songs, Op. 39, 1897**
2. SSA
3. Shakespeare
5. Schmidt

**0088 Three Songs, Op. 57,
1904**
2. SSA
5. Schmidt; Ditson

**0089 Through the House Give
Glimmering Light, Op. 39,
No. 3**
2. SSAA, piano
3. Shakespeare
5. Schmidt, 1897

**0090 We Who Sing, Op. 140,
1933**
2. SATB, piano
3. Amy Sherman Bridgeman
5. Ditson, 1934

**0091 When the Last Sea is
Sailed, Op. 127, 1931**
2. TTBB
3. John Masefield
5. Schmidt, 1931

**0092 With Prayer and
Supplication: see
Responses.**

**0093 Wouldn't That be
Queer? Op. 26, No. 4,
1894**
2. SSA, piano

BEACH

3. Elsie J. Cooley
5. Schmidt, 1919

0094 The Year's at the
Spring, Op. 44, No. 1
2. SSAA, piano
3. Robert Browning
5. Schmidt, 1909

0095 same for SA
5. Schmidt, 1919

0096 same for SATB
5. Schmidt, 1927

0097 The Yellow Daisy: see
Three Flower Songs.

B R A D B U R Y

0098 According To Thy Name
2. SATB
6. L of C

0099 And It Shall Come to
Pass in the Last Days
2. SATB
6. L of C

0100 (autograph)
2. SATB
3. no text
6. L of C

0101 As the Heart Panteth
5. in "The Triumph" by G.
F. Root, 1872 (Cin-
cinnati)
6. facsimile of autograph
in NYPL

0102 Awake, Put on Thy
Strength
2. SATB
3. biblical
6. L of C

0103 The Blessed In-
vitation
2. SATB
6. L of C

0104 Call John!, 1904
2. SATB
6. L of C

0105 Daniel: see listing
under same title by G. F.
Root (joint composer).
7. 069

0106 Double Fugue, 1848
2. SATB
6. L of C

0107 Esther, the Beautiful
Queen
2. SATB soli, SATB,
narrator, orchestra
3. Chauncey Marrin Cady
4. 45 minutes
5. Ditson, 1856, 1874,
1896; Mason, 1856;
Biglow and Main, 1884
7. 069

0108 Even Me
2. SATB
3. Elizabeth Condor

BRADBURY

5. Martin and Morris, 1946

0109   The Gospel Call
2. SATB
6. L of C

0110   He Leadeth Me
2. SSA
3. Joseph Henry Gilmore
5. Belwin,Inc., 1951; Empire
    Music Publ., 1952; Hill
    and Range Songs, Inc.,
    1952; R.D. Row, 1955;
    Southern Music, 1955

0111   Just As I Am
2. A or Bar solo, SSA
3. Charlotte Elliott
5. Belwin, Inc., 1949;
    Broadman Press, 1952

0112   Mein Vaterland, 1848
2. SATB
6. L of C

0113   Motette: Psalm 74, 1848
2. SATB
3. biblical
6. L of C

0114   Sweet Rivers
2. SATB
6. L of C

0115   Trust in God
2. SATB
6. L of C

B R I S T O W

0116   Benedic anima mea:
    see An Evening Service.

0117   Benedictus: see
    Morning Service, 1873

0118   The Bold Bad Barron,
    Op. 87, 1887
2. TTBB
6. New York Public Lib.

0119   Bonum est: see An
    Evening Service.

0120   Burial Service, Op. 34
2. SATB
3. biblical
6. New York Public Lib.

0121   Call John
2. SATB
6. New York Public Lib.

0122   Christ Our Passover,
    An Easter Anthem, Op. 39
2. SATB soli, SATB, organ
3. biblical
5. Wm. A Pond, 1875
6. New York Public Lib.

0123   Christmas Anthem, Op.
    73, 1887
2. SATB soli, SATB, organ
3. Jackson Elmendorf
6. New York Public Lib.

BRISTOW

0124 Daniel, Op. 42, 1866
2. SATB soli, SATB,
   orchestra
3. W.A. Hardenbrook;
   biblical
4. 60 minutes
5. publ. by composer, 1867
6. New York Public Lib.
7. 030

0125 Easter Anthem
2. SATB soli, SATB, organ
3. N.P. Beers
6. New York Public Lib.

0126 An Evening Service in
   D, Op. 36, 1863
2. SATB, organ
3. biblical
4. 12 minutes
5. Wm. A. Pond
6. New York Public Lib.
   a. Bonum est
   b. Benedic anima mea

0127 Evening Service in G
2. SATB
3. biblical
5. Grand Conservatory Publ.
6. New York Public Lib.

0128 The Great Republic, Ode
to the American Union, Op.
47, 1880
2. SATB soli, SATB,
   orchestra
3. William Oland Bourne
5. Biglow and Main, 1880
6. Newberry Lib. (holo-
   graph); New York Public
   Lib. (autograph); L of C
   (autograph)
7. 021

0129 Jubilate: see Morning
Service, Op. 19.

0130 Kyrie Eleison: see
Morning Service, Op. 19

0131 Light Flashing into
the Darkness: see Christ-
mas Anthem.

0132 Mass in C, Op. 57,
1885
2. SATB, orchestra
3. liturgical
4. 20 minutes
6. New York Public Lib.

0133 Morning Service, Op.
19, 1855?
2. SATB, organ
3. liturgical
4. 14 minutes
5. Saalfield
6. New York Public Lib.
   a. Te Deum in E-flat
   b. Jubilate in E-flat
   c. Kyrie eleison

0134 Morning Service, 1873
2. SAT soli, SATB, organ
3. biblical
4. 12 minutes
5. Wm. A. Pond
6. New York Public Lib.
   a. Te Deum in B-flat
   b. Benedictus

0135 Niagara, Op. 62, 189?
2. SATB, orchestra
4. 35-40 minutes
6. New York Public Lib.

BRISTOW

0136   O Beautiful Easter
Morn
2. SATB
6. L of C

0137   Ode written for G. S.,
No. 20, Op. 29, 1856
2. SATB soli, SATB,
orchestra
6. New York Public Lib.

0138   Offertories, Op. 48,
No. 1-3; Op. 1, No. 4
2. SATB
6. New York Public Lib.

0139   Peace, Goodwill, 1893
2. SATB
6. L of C

0140   The Pioneer, Op. 49,
1872
2. SATB soli, SATB,
orchestra
4. 15 minutes
6. New York Public Lib.
7. 030

0141   Praise to God, Op. 33,
1860
2. SATB soli, SATB,
orchestra
3. biblical (Te Deum text)
4. 40 minutes
5. Ditson, 1860
6. New York Public Lib.
7. 030

0142   Te Deum in E-flat: see
Morning Service, Op. 19.

0143   Te Deum in B-flat:
see   Morning Service,
1873.

B U C K

0144   Abu Ben Adhem: see Six
Three-Part Songs.

0145   Annie Laurie
2. SATB
3. P. Bachenberg
5. G. Schirmer, 1880

0146   Arise! Shine! For Thy
Light Has Come, Op. 53,
No. 6
2. SATB, organ
3. biblical
5. Buck's Second Motette
Collection; Ditson, 1871

0147   As It Began to Dawn,
Op. 72, No. 3
2. SATB, organ
3. biblical
5. G. Schirmer

0148   At Midnight: see Six
Songs for Male Voices.

0149   Ave Maria, Op. 9
2. S solo, SATB, orchestra
3. liturgical

0150   Bedtime: see Five
Three-Part Songs.

BUCK

0151   Behold, the Lamb of
God!
2.   SATB, organ
3.   Hymns Ancient and Modern
5.   Buck's Second Motette
Collection;   Ditson, 1871

0152   The Bells at Easter-
tide
2.   SATB
3.   W. H. Gardner
5.   Church, 1904

0153   Benedic anima: see
Evening Service, Op. 47.

0154   Benedic anima in B-
flat: see Evening Service,
Op. 31.

0155   Benedictus in C: see
Festival Morning Service.

0156   Benedictus in E-flat:
see Morning Service, Op.
25.

0157   Benedictus in E major:
see Te Deum in B Minor.

0158   Benedictus in A-flat:
see Morning Service.

0159   Benedictus in A-flat:
see Short Te Deum in E-
flat.

0160   Benedictus in A: see
Morning Service.

0161   Blessed Are the Dead
2.   SATB, organ
3.   biblical
5.   Buck's Motette
Collection; Ditson, 1864

0162   Bonum est: see
Evening Service, Op. 47.

0163   Bonum est in E-flat:
see Evening Service, Op.
64.

0164   Bonum est in B-flat:
Evening Service, Op. 31.

0165   Brightest and Best of
the Sons of the Morning
2.   SATB, organ
3.   biblical
5.   Buck's Motette Col-
lection; Ditson, 1864;
Presser, 1907

0166   Bugle Song, 1891
2.   TTBB, orchestra
3.   Alfred Lord Tennyson
4.   12-15 minutes
5.   G. Schirmer

0167   Cantate Domino: see
Evening Service.

0168   Cantate Domino in C:
see Evening Service, Op.
31.

0169   The Centennial Meditation of Columbia, 1879
2.   B solo, SATB, orchestra
3.   Sidney Lanier
4.   12 minutes
5.   G. Schirmer, 1876, 1904
6.   Conn. Historical Society
7.   010, 021, 123

BUCK

0170   Chorus of Spirits and
Hours, Op. 90, 1882
2.   T solo, TTBB, piano and
organ, strings and flute
ad lib.
3.   Percy Bysshe Shelley
4.   30-35 minutes
5.   G. Schirmer, 1882, 1905

0171   Christ Our Passover:
see Easter Anthem.

0172   Christ the Victor, 1896
2.   SATB soli, SATB, organ
3.   biblical; John Milton;
Harriet Auber
4.   20 minutes
5.   G. Schirmer, 1896

0173   The Christian Year:
see individual titles:
a.   The Triumph of David
b.   The Coming of the
King
c.   The Song of the
Night
d.   The Story of the
Cross
e.   Christ the Victor

0174   Christmas: see Three
Anthems.

0175   Christmas Anthem ("O
Zion That Tellest Good
Tidings"), Op. 48
2.   SATB, organ
3.   biblical
5.   G. Schirmer

0176   Christmas Anthem

("There Were Shepherds")
2.   SATB, organ
3.   biblical
5.   G. Schirmer, 1868?

0177   Come in the Stilly
Night: see Six Songs for
Male Voices.

0178   The Coming of the
King, 1895
2.   SATB soli, SATB div.,
congregation, organ
3.   biblical, arr. John
Byron
4.   40 minutes
5.   G. Schirmer, 1895
7.   069

0179   Communion Service in
C, 1893
2.   SATB
3.   liturgical
5.   G. Schirmer

0180   Concert Waltz: see
Five Four-Part Songs.

0181   Darkly Rose the Guilty
Morning, Op. 33
2.   SATB
5.   G. Schirmer, 1868

0182   Deus misereatur: see
Evening Service, Op. 47.

0183   Deus misereatur in A-
flat: see Evening Ser-
vice, Op. 64.

0184   Deus misereatur in B-
flat: see Evening Ser-
vice, Op. 31.

BUCK

0185 Easter: see Three
Anthems.

0186 Easter Anthem in B-
flat ("Christ Our Pass-
over"), Op. 46
2. SATB, organ
3. biblical
5. G. Schirmer, 1870

0187 Easter Morning, Op. 21
2. SSTB soli, SATB div.,
orchestra
3. Emmanuel Geibel (from
German)
4. 15 minutes
5. S. Brainard's Sons,
1865; Henry Tolman and
Co., 1865
7. 068

0188 Evening Hymn: see Five
Three-Part Songs.

0189 Evening Hymn, Op. 54,
No. 6
2. SATB, organ
3. Hymns Ancient and Modern
5. Buck's Second Motette
Collection; Ditson, 1871

0190 Evening Service, Op. 31
2. SATB, organ
3. biblical/liturgical
5. G. Schirmer, 1868, 1870
    a. Gloria in excelsis
       in B-flat
    b. Bonum est in B-flat
    c. Deus misereatur in
       B-flat
    d. Cantate Domino in C
    e. Benedic anima in B-
       flat

0191 Evening Service, Op.
47
2. SATB soli, SATB, organ
3. liturgical
5. G. Schirmer, 1870
    a. Gloria in excelsis
       ("Festival") in D
    b. Gloria in excelsis
       in G
    c. Bonum est
    d. Deus misereatur
    e. Cantate Domino
    f. Benedic anima

0192 Evening Service, Op.
64
2. SATB, organ
3. biblical/liturgical
4. 15 minutes
5. G. D. Russell, 1873;
   Ditson, n.d.
    a. Gloria in excelsis
       in A-flat
    b. Bonum est in E-flat
    c. Deus misereatur in
       A-flat

0193 Festival Hymn, Op. 57,
1872
2. SATB, piano
3. Dudley Buck
5. Ditson, 1900
6. Boston Public Lib.

0194 Festival Morning
Service
2. SATB, organ
3. biblical/liturgical
5. G. Schirmer, 1891
    a. Festival Te Deum,
       No. 9, in C
    b. Benedictus in C

0195 Festival Te Deum, No
9, in C: see Festival
Morning Service.

BUCK

0196 Festival Te Deum in E-
flat: see Morning Service.

0197 Festival Te Deum, No.
7, in E-flat and Jubilate
in B-flat, Op. 63
2. SATB, organ
3. liturgical
4. 17 minutes
5. G. D. Russell, 1873

0198 Five Four-Part Songs
for Male Voices, Op. 69
2. TTBB
5. G.D. Russell and Co.,
1875
   a. Concert Waltz
   b. The Star of Love
   c. Hark! The Trumpet
       Calleth
   d. Good Night!
   e. Lead, Kindly Light!

0199 Five Three-Part Songs,
1906
2. SSA, piano
3. (see below)
5. G. Schirmer
   a. (missing)
   b. Pretty Good World
       (anonymous)
   c. Evening Hymn (Dudley
       Buck)
   d. (missing)
   e. Bedtime (Burges
       Johnson)

0200 The Forty-Sixth Psalm,
Op. 57, 1872
2. STB soli, SATB div.,
orchestra
3. biblical
4. 40 minutes

5. Ditson, 1872, 1900
6. Boston Public Lib.
7. 039, 068
N.B.: first version, Op.
20, destroyed in fire; Op.
57 is a new version.

0201 Give Unto the Lord, O
Ye Mighty, Op. 53, No. 3
2. SATB, organ
3. biblical
5. Buck's Second Motette
Collection; Ditson, 1871

0202 Gloria in excelsis
("Festival") in D: see
Evening Service, Op. 47.

0203 Gloria in excelsis in
G: see Evening Service,
Op. 47.

0204 Gloria in excelsis in
A-flat: see Evening Ser-
vice, Op. 64.

0205 Gloria in excelsis in
B-flat: see Evening Ser-
vice, Op. 31.

0206 God is our Refuge:
see The Forty-Sixth Psalm.

0207 The God of Abraham
Praise, Op. 53, No. 1
2. SATB, organ
3. Thomas Olivers
5. Buck's Second Motette
Collection; Ditson,
1871

0208 same for TTBB
5. Ditson, 1913, 1935

BUCK

0209   God Who Madest Earth
and Heaven
2. SATB, organ
5. Ditson

0210   The Golden Legend: see
Scenes from the Golden
Legend.

0211   Good Friday: see Three
Anthems.

0212   Good Night!:   see Five
Four-Part Songs.

0213   The Grasshopper and the
Ant: see Six Three-Part
Songs.

0214   Gute Nacht: see Vier
Lieder für Männerstimmen.

0215   Hark! Hark! My Soul,
Op. 53, No. 2
2. SATB, organ
3. Hymns Ancient and Modern
5. Buck's Second Motette
Collection; Ditson, 1871

0216   Hark! The Trumpet
Calleth: see Five Four-
Part Songs.

0217   He Shall Come Down Like
Rain, Op. 53, No. 4
1. SATB, organ
3. biblical
5. Buck's Second Motette
Collection; Ditson, 1871

0218   Huzza! (Wine Song):
see Six Songs for Male
Voices.

0219   Hymn to Music, 1877
2. SSAATTBB
3. Charles J. Sprague
5. G. Schirmer, 1877, 1905

0220   I Will Call Upon Thee,
Op. 54, No. 3
2. SATB, organ
3. biblical
5. Buck's Second Motette
Collection; Ditson, 1871

0221   I Will Lift Up Mine
Eyes
2. SATB, organ
3. biblical
5. Buck's Motette Col-
lection; Ditson, 1864

0222   In Absence: see Six
Songs for Male Voices.

0223   Jubilate in C: see
Morning Service.

0224   Jubilate in C Major:
see Te Deum in C Major.

0225   Jubilate in E-flat:
see Morning Service, Op.
25.

0226   Jubilate in A: see
Morning Service.

0227   Jubilate in B-flat:

BUCK

see Festival Te Deum in E-
flat, No. 7.

0228   Jubilate in B-flat:
see Morning Service.

0229   Jubilate Deo
2.   SATB, organ
3.   biblical
5.   Buck's Motette Col-
     lection; Ditson, 1864

0230   King Olaf's Christmas,
Op. 86, 1881?
2.   TBar solo, TTBB, piano,
     reed organ and strings ad
     lib.; separate parts for
     winds, percussion
3.   Henry W. Longfellow
4.   30 minutes
5.   G. Schirmer, 1881, 1905
6.   New York Public Lib.

0231   Lead, Kindly Light!:
see Five Four-Part Songs.

0232   The Legend of Don
Munio, Op. 62, 1873-74
2.   SATB soli, SATB div.,
     orchestra
3.   Washington Irving; arr.
     Buck
4.   80 minutes
5.   Ditson, 1874, 1902
6.   Boston Public Lib.

0233   Light of Asia, 1886
2.   STB soli, SATB,
     orchestra
3.   Edwin Arnold
4.   60-70 minutes

5.   Novello, 1886
6.   University of Colorado
7.   099, 121

0234   Die linden Luffe sind
erwacht: see Vier Lieder
für Männerstimmen.

0235   The Lord is King
2.   SATB, organ
3.   biblical
5.   Buck's Motette Col-
     lection; Ditson, 1864

0236   Mein Vaterland: see
Vier Lieder für Männer-
stimmen.

0237   Midnight Service for
New Year's Eve, 1880
2.   SATB, organ
3.   liturgical
5.   G. Schirmer, 1880, 1908

0238   Morning Service
2.   SATB, organ
3.   liturgical
5.   Ditson
     a.   Te Deum in C
     b.   Jubilate in C
     c.   Te Deum in B minor
     d.   Benedictus in E
     e.   Te Deum in E-flat
     f.   Benedictus in A-flat
     g.   Festival Te Deum in
          E-flat
     h.   Jubilate in B-flat

0239   Morning Service, Op.
25
2.   SATB, organ
3.   biblical/liturgical
5.   G. Schirmer, 1868, 1870
     a.   Venite in E-flat
     b.   Te Deum in B-flat

BUCK

   c. Benedictus in E-flat
   d. Jubilate in E-flat

0240 **Morning Service**, Op. 45
2. SATB soli, SATB, organ
3. liturgical
5. G. Schirmer, 1875
   a. Venite in A
   b. Te Deum in D
   c. Te Deum ("Short")
   d. Jubilate in A
   e. Benedictus in A
   f. Sanctus and Kyrie

0241 **The Night Song of Bethlehem**
2. S or Bar solo, SATB, organ
3. biblical
5. G. Schirmer, 1903

0242 **Now From the Sixth Hour There Was Darkness**, Op. 72, No. 2
2. SATB, organ
3. biblical
5. G. Schirmer, 1876, 1904

0243 **The Nun of Nidaros**, Op. 83, 1879
2. T solo, TTBB, piano/organ ad lib., string quintet, flute
3. Henry W. Longfellow
4. 20 minutes
5. G. Schirmer, 1879, 1905
7. 069

0244 **O Clap Your Hands All Ye People**, Op. 54, No. 2
2. SATB, organ
3. biblical

5. Buck's Second Motette Collection; Ditson, 1871

0245 **O How Amiable**
2. SATB, organ
3. biblical
5. Buck's Motette Collection; Ditson, 1864; Presser, 1907

0246 **O Lord, Rebuke Me Not**, Op. 54, No. 1
2. SATB, organ
3. biblical
5. Buck's Second Motette Collection; Ditson, 1871

0247 **O Lord, Thou Art My God**, Op. 54, No. 5
2. SATB, organ
3. biblical
5. Buck's Second Motette Collection; Ditson, 1871

0248 **O Praise God in His Holiness**, Op. 54, No. 4
2. SATB, organ
3. biblical
5. Buck's Second Motette Collection; Ditson, 1871

0249 **O Thou Afflicted**, Op. 53, No. 5
2. SATB, organ
3. biblical
5. Buck's Second Motette Collection; Ditson, 1871

0250 **O Zion That Tellest Good Tidings**: see **Christmas Anthem**.

0251 **On the Sea**: see **Six Three-Part Songs**.

BUCK

0252 On Tree Top: see Six
Songs for Male Voices.

0253 Out of the Deeps
2. SATB, organ
3. biblical
5. Buck's Motette Col-
lection; Ditson, 1864

0254 Our Motto, 1895
2. TTBB

0255 Paul Revere's Ride,
1898
2. TBar soli, TTBB,
orchestra
3. Henry W. Longfellow
4. 20 minutes
5. G. Schirmer, 1898, 1905

0256 Peace, Troubled Soul
2. SATB, organ
5. Buck's Motette Col-
lection; Ditson, 1864

0257 Pretty Good World: see
Five Three-Part Songs.

0258 Prometheus Unbound
2. T solo, TTBB, piano,
reed organ, string
quintet, flute
3. Percy Bysshe Shelley
5. G. Schirmer, 1882

0259 Reise des Columbus:
see The Voyage of Columbus.

0260 Sanctus: see Six

Three-Part Songs.

0261 Sanctus and Kyrie:
see Morning Service.

0262 Scenes from the Golden
Legend, 1880
2. SATB soli, SATB,
orchestra
3. Henry W. Longfellow
4. 45-50 minutes
5. Church, 1880, 1908
6. L of C
7. 121

0263 She is Mine!:   see Six
Songs for Male Voices.

0264 Short Te Deum in E-
flat, No. 6 and Benedictus
in A-flat, Op. 61
2. SATB, organ
3. liturgical
4. 15 minutes
5. G. D. Russell, 1873

0265 Sing Alleluia Forth
2. TTBB, organ
5. Ditson, 1901, 1908

0266 Sing Hosanna in the
Highest
2. SATB, organ
3. biblical
5. G. Schirmer, 1906

0267 Six Cantatas for Men's
Voices: see individual
titles:
  a. The Nun of Nidaros
  b. King Olaf's Christ-
mas
  c. Chorus of Spirits

BUCK

      and Hours
  d. The Voyage of
     Columbus
  e. Bugle Song
  f. Paul Revere's Ride

0268 Six Songs for Male
  Voices, Op. 55
2. TTBB
3. see below
5. Ditson
  a. Huzza! (Wine Song)
  b. In Absence
  c. Come in the Stilly
    Night
  d. At Midnight (R.
    Reinick)
  e. On Tree Top
  f. She Is Mine!

0269 Six Three-part Songs
  for Women's or Boy's
  voices, 1908
2. SSA, piano
3. see below
5. G. Schirmer
  a. Abu Ben Adhem (Leigh
    Hunt)
  b. Wanderer's Night
    Song (Buck, after
    Goethe)
  c. The Grasshopper and
    the Ant (after La
    Fontaine)
  d. Spring's Welcome
    (Buck)
  e. On the Sea (Buck)
  f. Sanctus (liturgical)

0270 The Song of the Drum,
  1902
2. TTBB
5. G. Schirmer

0271 Song of the Flag, 1894
2. SATB
3. Richard Burton
5. Case, Lockwood, and
   Brainard Co.

0272 The Song of the Night
2. SATB soli, SATB, organ
5. G. Schirmer

0273 Spring's Welcome: see
  Six Three-Part Songs.

0274 The Star of Love: see
  Five Four-Part Songs.

0275 The Story of the
  Cross, 1892
2. SATB soli, SATB,
   orchestra
3. Buck
4. 45-50 minutes
5. G. Schirmer, 1892
7. 069

0276 A Summer Night, 1880
2. TTBB
3. R. Reinick
5. Wm. A. Pond, 1880

0277 Te Deum ("Short"): see
  Morning Service.

0278 Te Deum in C: see
  Morning Service.

0279 Te Deum in C Major
  (No. 4) and Jubilate in C
  Major, Op. 58
2. SATB, organ
3. liturgical
4. 15 minutes
5. G. D. Russell, 1872

BUCK

c. Easter (10 minutes)

0280   Te Deum in D: see
Morning Service.

0281   Te Deum in E-flat: see
Morning Service.

0282   Te Deum in B-flat: see
Morning Service, Op. 25.

0283   Te Deum in B Minor:
see Morning Service.

0284   Te Deum in B Minor (No.
5) and Benedictus in E Major, Op. 60
2. SATB, organ
3. liturgical
4. 15 minutes
5. G. D. Russell, 1872

0285   There Was Darkness, Op.
72, No. 1
2. SATB, organ
5. G. Schirmer, 1868

0286   Thou Wilt Keep Him in
Perfect Peace
2. SATB, organ
3. biblical
5. Buck's Motette Col-
lection; Ditson, 1864

0287   Three Anthems, Op. 72,
1876
2. SATB soli, SATB, organ
3. biblical
4. (see below)
5. G. Schirmer
a. Christmas
b. Good Friday

0288   The Triumph of David,
1892
2. SATB soli, SATB, organ
3. Buck
4. 25 minutes
5. G. Schirmer, 1893, 1912
6. L of C
7. 034, 069

0289   Venite in A: see
Morning Service.

0290   Venite in E-flat: see
Morning Service, Op. 25.

0291   Vier Lieder für
Männerstimmen, Op. 3
2. TTBB
5. unpublished
6. mss. destroyed
a. Willst du von dem
Lenze singen
b. Mein Vaterland
c. Gute Nacht
d. Die linden Luffe
sind erwacht

0292   The Voyage of
Columbus, 1885
2. TTB soli, TTBB,
orchestra
3. Buck, after Washington
Irving
4. 60 minutes
5. G. Schirmer, 1885, 1905
7. 021, 122

0293   Wanderer's Night Song:
see Six Three-Part Songs.

0294   The Warrior's Death,
1884

BUCK

2. Bar solo, TTBB
3. L. Liebe
6. L of C

0295 When the Lord Turned
Again the Captivity of Zion
2. SATB, organ
3. biblical
5. Buck's Motette Col-
lection; Ditson, 1864;
Presser, 1907

0296 Willst du von dem Lenze
singen: see Vier Lieder
für Männerstimmen.

C H A D W I C K

0297 Abide with Me, 1888
2. SATB
5. Schmidt, 1888

0298 Art Thou Weary?, 1890
2. SATB
5. Schmidt

0299 As the Hart Pants: see
Three Sacred Quartettes.

0300 At the Bride's Gate:
see Three Choruses.

0301 The Autumn Winds: see
Four Songs of Brittany.

0302 Awake Up, My Glory,
1895
2. SATB
5. Schmidt

0303 The Beatitudes, 1895
2. SATB, organ
5. Schmidt

0304 Behind the Lattice:
see Two Four-Part Songs.

0305 Behold the Works of
the Lord, 1891
2. SATB
5. Schmidt

0306 Blessed Be the Lord:
see Three Sacred Anthems.

0307 The Bluebells of New
England, 1917
2. SSA, piano
3. Thomas Bailey Aldrich
5. Ditson, 1917

0308 The Boy and the Owl,
1886
2. TTBB
5. Schmidt

0309 Brightest and Best,
1888
2. SATB
5. Schmidt

0310 Buie Annajohn
2. SATB, piano
3. Bliss Carmen
5. A Book of Choruses,
Silver Burdett, 1923

CHADWICK

0311 Caravan Song
2. SATB, piano
3. Alfred H. Hyatt
5. A Book of Choruses,
    Silver Burdett, 1923

0312 Chorus of Pilgrim Women
2. SSAA, piano
3. The Pilgrim Pageant
5. A Book of Choruses,
    Silver Burdett, 1923

0313 A Christmas Greeting
2. SATB
6. New England Cons.
    (holograph); L of C
    (autograph facsimile)

0314 Columbia, 1892, rev.
    1907
2. SSAATTBB, orchestra
4. 25 minutes
6. L of C

0315 Come Hither, Ye
    Faithful, 1891
5. Schmidt

0316 Come Unto Me, 1904
2. SATB, organ
5. G. Schirmer, 1904

0317 Commemoration Ode
2. SATB, piano
3. James Russell Lowell
4. 10 minutes
5. Ditson, 1928
6. New England Cons.

0318 Credo: see Three

Partsongs.

0319 Darest Thou Now, O
    Soul: see Three Partsongs.

0320 Dedication Ode, Op.
    15, 1886
2. SATB soli, SATB,
    orchestra
3. Henry Bernard Carpenter
5. Schmidt, 1886
6. New England Cons.
7. 070

0321 Deep in the Soul of a
Rose
2. SSA, piano
3. Alfred H. Hyatt
5. A Book of Choruses,
    Silver Burdett, 1923

0322 Dolly, 1917
2. SSA, piano
3. Austin Dobson
5. Ditson

0323 Dorcas: see Three
    Choruses.

0324 Drinking Song, 1886
2. TTBB
5. Schmidt

0325 Ecce iam noctis, 1897
2. TTBB, organ, orchestra
3. from hymn by Gregory;
    trans. Isabella Parker
4. 10 minutes
5. Schmidt, 1897
6. L of C

0326 Elfin Song, 1910
2. SSAA, piano

CHADWICK

3. Joseph R. Drake
5. Schmidt
6. New England Cons.

0327 Evening
2. SATB, piano
3. S. Baring-Gould
5. Ditson, 1927
6. L of C

0328 Fathers of the Free
2. SATB, piano
3. Elmer Ellsworth Brown
5. H. W. Gray Co., 1927, 1928
6. New England Cons.

0329 Four Songs of Brittany, 1890
2. SSAA
5. Schmidt
    a. The Autumn Wind
    b. Love Is Fleeting
    c. My Sweetheart Gave
    d. The Lark That Sang

0330 God To Whom We Look Up Blindly: see Three Sacred Quartettes.

0331 God Who Madest Earth and Heaven: see Three Sacred Quartettes.

0332 Hail Us Doctors of Song, 1914
2. TTBB
5. Sängerfest

0333 Hark, Hark, My Soul,

1903
2. A solo, SATB
3. Frederick W. Faber
5. G. Schirmer, 1903

0334 The Immortal, 1923
2. SATB, piano
3. Cale Young Rice
5. C.C. Birchard, 1923

0335 In a China Shop, 1910
2. SSAA, piano
3. George C. Hellman
5. Schmidt, 1910

0336 Inconstancy, 1910
2. SSAA, piano
3. Shakespeare
5. Schmidt, 1910

0337 same for TTBB
5. Schmidt, 1910

0338 It Was a Lover, 1910
2. TTBB, piano
3. Shakespeare
5. Schmidt, 1910

0339 same for SSAA
5. Schmidt, 1910

0340 Jabberwocky, 1887
2. TTBB
5. Schmidt

0341 Jehovah Reigns in Majesty, 1916
2. TTBB, orchestra
3. biblical
5. Ditson, 1916
6. New England Cons. (parts only; no full score extant)

CHADWICK

0342   Joshua, 1919
2.   TTBB, piano
3.   R. D. Ware
5.   Ditson, 1919
6.   New England Cons.

0343   Jubilate in B-flat, 1895
2.   SATB, organ
5.   Schmidt

0344   Judith, 1900-01
2.   SATB soli, SATB, orchestra
3.   William Chauncey Langdon
4.   90 minutes
5.   G. Schirmer, 1901; Da Capo, 1972
6.   L of C
7.   032, 069
N.B.: classified by many writers as an opera

0345   June, 1918
2.   SSA, piano
3.   Justin H. Smith
5.   Ditson, 1918

0346   Land of Our Hearts, 1918
2.   SSAATTBB, orchestra
3.   John Hall Ingham
4.   20 minutes
5.   Boston Music Co., 1918; A Book of Choruses, Silver Burdett, 1923
6.   L of C

0347   The Lark that Sang: see Four Songs of Brittany.

0348   Lied des Viking

6.   New England Cons.

0349   The Lily Nymph, 1893, rev. 1895?
2.   STB soli, SATB, orchestra
3.   Arlo Bates
4.   60-70 minutes
5.   Schmidt, 1895
6.   L of C

0350   The Little Lac Grenier
2.   SATB, piano
3.   William Henry Drummond
5.   A Book of Choruses, Silver Burdett, 1923

0351   Lord of All Power and Might, 1895
2.   SATB, organ
3.   biblical
5.   Schmidt, 1895

0352   Love Is Fleeting: see Four Songs of Brittany.

0353   Lovely Rosabelle, 1889
2.   ST soli, SATB, orchestra
3.   Sir Walter Scott
4.   18 minutes
5.   Schmidt, 1889
6.   New England Cons.; L of C (sketches)
7.   100

0354   Lullaby
2.   SSAA
5.   Schmidt, 1889

0355   A Madrigal for Christmas
2.   SATB
6.   L of C

CHADWICK

0356 Margarita
2. TTBB
3. Scheffel
5. Schmidt, 1881, 1909

0357 Mary's Lullaby, 1910
2. SSAA, piano
3. Cora A. Matoon Dolson
5. Schmidt, 1910

0358 A May Carol
2. SATB, piano
3. Frank Dempster Sherman
5. Ditson, 1927
6. L of C

0359 Mexican Serenade, 1921
2. SATB, piano
3. Arthur Guiterman (Arline Guitelman?)
5. A Book of Choruses, Silver Burdett, 1923
6. New England Cons.

0360 Miss Nancy's Gown, 1910
2. SSAA, piano
3. Zitella Cooke
5. Schmidt, 1910

0361 Mister Moon
2. SSAA, piano
3. Bliss Carmen
5. A Book of Choruses, Silver Burdett, 1923

0362 Morn's Roseate Hues, 1903
2. SATB
3. The Hymnal
5. Novello, 1903

0363 My Sweetheart Gave: see Four Songs of Brittany.

0364 The New Hail Columbia, 1895
2. Bar solo, TTBB, piano
3. W. Murdoch Lind
5. B.F. Wood, 1917

0365 Nöel, 1888
2. SATB soli, SATB, orchestra
3. various sources
4. 40 minutes
5. H. W. Gray, 1909; Novello, 1909
6. L of C
7. 026, 069

0366 O Cease, My Wandering Soul, 1888
2. SATB, organ
5. Schmidt, 1888

0367 O Day of Rest, 1888
2. SATB
5. Schmidt

0368 O God, Be Merciful, 1890
2. SATB
5. Schmidt

0369 O Holy Child of Bethlehem, 1896
2. A solo, SATB
3. Phillips Brooks
5. Schmidt, 1896

0370 O Thou That Hearest: see Three Sacred Anthems.

CHADWICK

0371 Ode for the Opening of
   the Chicago World's Fair,
   1892
2. ST soli, SATB, orchestra
3. Harriet Monroe
4. 30-35 minutes
5. J. Church, 1892
7. 087

0372 Pack, Clouds, Away:
   see Three Partsongs.

0373 Peace and Light, 1895
2. SATB
5. Schmidt, 1895

0374 Phoenix Expirans, 1892
2. SATB soli, SATB,
   orchestra
3. John Lord Hayes
4. 25 minutes
5. Schmidt, 1892
6. Springfield, Mass., City
   Lib. (score); New
   England Cons. (mss.
   parts); L of C (holo-
   graph sketches)

0375 The Pilgrims, 1891
2. SATB, orchestra
3. Felicia Dorothea Browne
   Hemans
4. 15 minutes
5. Schmidt, 1890
6. New England Cons.
7. 069

0376 Praise the Lord: see
   Three Sacred Anthems.

0377 Prayer, 1889
2. SATB
5. Schmidt

0378 Psalm 99: see Jehovah
   Reigns in Majesty.

0379 Reiterlied, 1881
2. TTBB
5. Schmidt, 1881, 1909

0380 Rondel: see Two Four-
   Part Choruses, 1903.

0381 The Runaway
2. SATB, piano
3. Cale Young Rice
5. Ditson, 1927
6. L of C

0382 Sängerfest Lied
2. TTBB, piano
3. John Koren
5. Sängerfest, 1914

0383 Saint Botolph, 1929
2. TTBB, piano or organ
3. Arthur Macy
5. B. F. Wood, 1913;
   Ditson, 1929
6. L of C

0384 Salute the Sacred
   Dead, 1928
2. SATB
5. Ditson

0385 Saviour, Again to Thy
   Dear Name, 1904
2. SATB, piano or organ
3. John Ellerton
5. Novello, 1904

0386 Saviour, Like a
   Shepherd, 1891
2. SATB
5. Schmidt

CHADWICK

0387   Sentences and
Responses, 1985
2.   SATB, organ
5.   Schmidt

0388   Serenade, 1886
2.   TTBB
5.   Schmidt

0389   Shout, Ye High Heavens,
1897
2.   SATB
3.   John Lord Hayes
5.   Schmidt, 1897

0390   Silently Swaying, 1916
2.   SSAA, piano
3.   V. von Scheffel
5.   Ditson, 1916
6.   New England Cons.

0391   Song of the Viking,
1882
2.   TTBB, orchestra
3.   L. T. Craigin
4.   11 minutes
5.   Schmidt, 1881

0392   The Spring Beauties,
1911
2.   SSA, piano
3.   Helen Gray Cone
5.   Schmidt, 1911

0393   Spring Song, Op. 9,
1882
2.   SSAA, piano
5.   Schmidt, 1882

0394   Stabat Mater: see Two

Four-Part Choruses, 1902.

0395   Sun of My Soul, 1904
2.   T solo, SATB
3.   John Keble
5.   Novello, 1904

0396   Teach Me, O Lord, 1903
2.   SATB
5.   Ditson

0397   There Were Shepherds,
1888
2.   SATB
5.   Schmidt

0398   These to the Front,
1918
2.   TTBB, piano
3.   M.A. de Wolfe Howe
5.   Ditson, 1918

0399   Thistledown: see Two
Four-Part Choruses.

0400   Thou Shalt Love the
Lord the God, 1904
2.   SATB
5.   G. Schirmer, 1904

0401   Thou Who Art Love
Divine, 1895
2.   SATB
3.   O.B. Brown
5.   Schmidt, 1895

0402   Three Choruses, 1904
2.   SSAA
5.   G. Schirmer, 1904
   a.   To Heliodora
   b.   At the Bride's Gate
   c.   Dorcas

CHADWICK

0403   Three Partsongs, 1910
2. TTBB
3. see below
5. Schmidt, 1910
    a. Darest Thou Now, O
        Soul (Walt Whitman)
    b. Credo (Thackeray)
    c. Pack, Clouds, Away
        (Thomas Heywood)

0404   Three Sacred Anthems,
    Op. 6, 1882
2. SATB
5. Schmidt
    a. Praise the Lord
    b. Blessed Be the Lord
    c. O Thou That Hearest

0405   Three Sacred Quartettes
2. SATB, organ
5. Schmidt, 1885
    a. As the Hart Pants
    b. God Who Madest Earth
        and Heaven
    c. God To Whom We Look
        Up Blindly

0406   To Heliodora: see
    Three Choruses.

0407   Two Four-Part Choruses,
    1902
2. SSAA
3. see below
5. G. Schirmer, 1902
    a. Stabat Mater
        (Giacopone)
    b. Thistledown (Arthur
        Macy)

0408   Two Four-Part Choruses,
    1903

2. SSAA
3. see below
5. G. Schirmer, 1903
    a. Rondel (J.C. Grant)
    b. Behind the Lattice
        (S.M. Peck)

0409   The Viking's Last
    Voyage, 1881
2. Bar solo, TTBB,
    orchestra
3. Sylvester Baxter
4. 20 minutes
5. Schmidt, 1881, 1909
6. New England Cons.

0410   Welcome Happy Morn,
    1895
2. SATB
5. Schmidt

0411   What Say?
2. SATB, piano
3. Grace F. Norton
5. Ditson, 1927
6. L of C

0412   When I View the Mother
    Holding, 1909
2. SSAA
5. H. W. Gray, 1909

0413   When Love Was Young,
    1886
2. TTBB
5. Schmidt

0414   When the Lord of Love
    Was Here, 1895
2. SATB
5. Schmidt

CHADWICK

0415 While Shepherds
Watched, 1899
2. SATB, organ
5. Schmidt, 1889

0416 While Thee I Seek, 1891
2. SATB
5. Schmidt

CLARKE

0417 The Garden Lily and the
Meadow Flowers
2. equal voices
4. 10 minutes
5. Ginn and Co., 1898

0418 Jerusalem, 1890
2. SATB soli, SATB,
orchestra
3. biblical
4. 90 minutes
5. Presser, 1890

0419 The Music of the
Spheres, 1880
2. TTBB
5. Presser

0420 Music to Aristophanes'
Acharnians, 1886
2. TTBB, piano
3. Aristophanes
4. 20 minutes
5. Clare, 1886

0421 Philadelphia Historical
Pageant, 1912
2. SATB, orchestra
5. Presser

FOOTE

0422 And There Were Shepherds in the Same Country,
1893
2. soli, SATB, organ
3. biblical
5. Schmidt, 1893, 1920/21
6. unknown

0423 Arise! Shine!
2. soli, SATB, organ
3. biblical
5. Schmidt, 1897, 1924-25;
Curwen, 1904
6. L of C

0424 Awake! Thou That
Sleepest
2. soli, SATB, organ
3. biblical
5. Schmidt, 1897, 1924-25
6. L of C

0425 Be Thou My Guide
2. SATB, organ
5. Schmidt, 1915
6. L of C (incomplete)

0426 The Beatitudes: see
Responses for Church Use.

0427 Beautiful Star in the
East

FOOTE

2. unison voices, piano
3. Mrs. G. F. Pinkham
5. Ditson

0428 Bedouin Song
2. TTBB, orchestra
3. Bayard Taylor
5. Schmidt, 1892, 1920;
   Breitkopf, 1907
6. L of C

0429 same for SATB
5. Schmidt, 1903, 1930-31

0430 same for TTBB
5. Schmidt

0431 Beloved, Let Us Love
One Another: see Responses
for Church Use.

0432 Benedicite omnia opera
in E
2. SATB, organ
3. liturgical
5. Schmidt, 1892, 1920
6. L of C

0433 Benedictus in E-flat
2. SATB, organ
3. liturgical
5. Schmidt, 1892, 1920
6. L of C

0434 Bugle Song (The Splen-
dour Falls on Castle Walls)
2. TTBB, piano
3. Alfred Lord Tennyson
5. Schmidt, 1895, 1922;
   Breitkopf, 1907

6. L of C

0435 A Canadian Boat Song
2. SATB, piano
3. Thomas Moore
5. A Book of Choruses,
   Silver Burdett, 1923

0436 The Cardinal Flower:
see Flower Songs.

0437 The Children of Is-
rael: see Music of the
Synagogue.

0438 Christ Our Passover
2. SATB soli, SATB, organ
3. biblical
5. Schmidt, 1894
6. L of C

0439 The Columbine: see
Flower Songs.

0440 Come, Live With Me and
Be My Love.
2. SA
3. Christopher Marlowe
5. Schmidt, 1889, 1917;
   Breitkopf, 1907
6. unknown

0441 Constancy
2. SSAA
3. anonymous
5. Schmidt, 1928

0442 The Crocus: see
Flower Songs.

FOOTE

Foxglove," a vocal solo.

0443 Crossing the Bar
2. TTBB
3. Alfred Lord Tennyson
5. Schmidt, 1897, 1924-25;
   Breitkopf, 1907
6. unknown

0444 Does the Road Wind
   Uphill All the Way?
2. solo, SATB, piano
3. Christina Rossetti
5. Schmidt, 1903, 1930
6. L of C

0445 The Farewell of
   Hiawatha, Op. 11, 1885
2. B solo, TTBB, orchestra
3. Henry W. Longfellow
4. 15 minutes
5. Schmidt, 1886, 1913-14
6. L of C (vocal score);
   Harvard Musical Assoc.
   (full score)
7. 021, 122

0446 Farewell to Summer
2. TTBB
3. Agnes Lockhart Hughes
5. Schmidt, 1911
6. L of C

0447 Flower Songs, Op. 49,
   1901?
2. SSAA, piano
3. Arlo Bates
4. 15 minutes (total)
5. Schmidt, 1902, 1929
6. L of C
   a. The Trilliums
   b. The Crocus
   c. The Meadowrue
   d. The Columbine
   e. The Cardinal Flower
N.B.: also includes "The

0448 Four Songs, Op. 68
2. SATB
3. see below
4. 20 minutes
5. Schmidt, 1908, 1935
6. L of C
   a. Too Soon So Fair,
      Fair Lilies (Augusta
      Webster)
   b. The Wind and the Day
      (Andrew Lang)
   c. Scythe Song (Lang)
   d. The Jumblies (Edward
      Lear)

0449 The Gateway of
   Ispahan, 1914
2. SSA, orchestra
3. Arlo Bates
5. Schmidt, 1914
6. L of C (vocal score);
   New England Cons. (full
   score)

0450 God Is Our Refuge and
   Strength
2. S or T solo, SATB, organ
3. biblical
5. H.W. Gray/Novello, 1889
6. unknown

0451 Gray Twilight
2. SSA
3. Agnes Lockhart Hughes
5. Schmidt, 1909, 1937;
   Breitkopf, 1913
6. L of C

0452 The Green of Spring
2. SSAA
3. Helen Hawley
5. Schmidt, 1906, 1933;
   Breitkopf, 1908

FOOTE

0453   Hear, Israel: see Music
for the Synagogue.

0454   Hear My Prayer, O God
2.   TTBB, organ
3.   biblical
5.   Schmidt, 1914
6.   L of C

0455   His Glory is in the
Earth and the Heavens: see
Music for the Synagogue.

0456   Holy, Holy: see Music
for the Synagogue.

0457   I Cannot Find Thee,
1904
2.   SATB, organ
3.   Eliza Schudder
5.   Schmidt, 1904, 1932
6.   L of C

0458   I Love My Love
2.   TTBB
3.   Charles MacKay
5.   Schmidt, 1892, 1920
6.   L of C

0459   I Will Arise and Go To
My Father: see Responses
for Church Use.

0460   If Doughty Deeds My
Lady Please, 1884
2.   TTBB
3.   Graham of Gartmore
5.   Schmidt, 1885, 1912-13
6.   L of C

0461   If Thou But Suffer God
To Guide Thee
2.   solo, ATB, organ
3.   Georg Neumark, trans.
Catherine Winkworth
5.   Schmidt, 1904, 1932
6.   L of C

0462   same for SATB
5.   Schmidt, 1915

0463   Into the Silent Land,
1886
2.   TTBB
3.   Johann Gaudenz Salis,
trans. Henry W. Long-
fellow
5.   Schmidt, 1886, 1896,
1924; Breitkopf, 1907
6.   unknown

0464   same for SATB
5.   Schmidt, 1897, 1924
6.   L of C

0465   same for SSAA
5.   Schmidt, 1889, 1917
6.   L of C

0466   It Is a Tree of Life:
see Music for the Syna-
gogue.

0467   It Is Good to Give
Thanks: see Music for the
Synagogue.

0468   An Irish Folk Song,
1905
2.   TTBB, piano
3.   Sir Gilbert Parker
5.   Schmidt, 1905, 1932;
Boosey and Co., 1909
6.   L of C

FOOTE

0469   same for SATB
5. Schmidt, 1900, 1927

0470   same for SSAA
5. Schmidt, 1905, 1932
6. L of C

0471   Jubilate in E-flat
Major: see Te Deum and
Jubilate, Op. 7

0472   Jubilate in A-flat
Major
2. SATB, organ
3. liturgical
5. Schmidt, 1894, 1921-22
6. L of C

0473   The Jumblies: see Four
Songs.

0474   The Law of the Lord is
Perfect
2. soli, SATB, organ
3. biblical
5. Schmidt, 1904, 1931
6. L of C

0475   Lift Up Your Heads:
see Music for the Syna-
gogue.

0476   Listen, O Isles, Unto
Me
2. soli, SATB, organ
5. Schmidt, 1911
6. L of C

0477   The Little Creek Goes
Winding

2. SSA, piano
3. John Bernard O'Hara
5. Schmidt, 1912
6. L of C

0478   The Lord of All Did
Reign: see Music for the
Synagogue.

0479   Lord of the Worlds
Above
2. soli, SAB, organ
3. biblical paraphrase by
Isaac Watts
5. Schmidt, 1899, 1926
6. L of C

0480   The Lord Will Reign:
see Music for the Syna-
gogue.

0481   The Lord's Prayer
2. SATB, organ
3. biblical
5. Schmidt, 1896, 1906,
1924; Curwen, 1896
6. unknown

0482   Love Has Turned His
Face Away
2. SSA, piano
3. Philip Bourke Marston
5. Schmidt, 1929
6. L of C

0483   Love Me, If I Live!,
1920
2. SSA, piano
3. Barry Cornwall
5. Schmidt, 1921
6. L of C

0484   Lygeia, Op. 58, 1907

FOOTE

2. SA soli, SSAA, orchestra
3. Gertrude Rogers
4. 45 minutes
5. Schmidt, 1906, 1933
6. New York Public Lib.

0485   Magnificat
2. TTBB, organ or piano
3. biblical
5. Schmidt, 1915
6. L of C

0486   Magnificat and Nunc dimittis in B-flat
2. SATB, organ
3. liturgical
5. Schmidt, 1892, 1920
6. L of C

0487   The Meadowrue: see Flower Songs.

0488   May the Words of My Mouth: see Music for the Synagogue.

0489   The Miller's Daughter, 1902?
2. TTBB
3. Alfred Lord Tennyson
5. Schmidt, 1901
6. L of C

0490   Mortal Life is Full of Battle: see Vita nostra plena bellis.

0491   Mount Carmel
2. SSAA, organ
3. Caroline Hazard

5. Schmidt, 1909, 1936-37; Breitkopf, 1910
6. L of C

0492   The Munster Fusiliers, 1918?
2. TTBB, orchestra
3. N. H. Gubbins (N. R. Seebins?)
5. Schmidt, 1918, 1945
6. New England Cons. (full score); L of C (vocal score)

0493   Music for the Synagogue, Op. 53, 1902
2. cantor, SATB soli, SATB, organ
3. biblical (transliterated Hebrew)
5. Schmidt, 1902, 1936
   a. It Is Good to Give Thanks
   b. Praise the Lord
   c. Hear, Israel
   d. Praised Be His Holy Name
   e. Who Is Like Unto Thee
   f. Sanctification
   g. Holy, Holy
   h. The Lord Will Reign
   i. May the Words of My Mouth
   j. Lift Up Your Heads
   k. Thine, O Lord, Is the Greatness
   l. His Glory Is in the Earth and the Heavens
   m. It Is a Tree of Life
   n. We Bend the Knee
   o. The Lord of All Did Reign
   p. The Children of Israel
   q. Responses for the Third Sabbath of the

FOOTE

    Month
  r. My Strength Is in the
      Lord

0494 My Strength Is In the
Lord: see Music for the
Synagogue.

0495 The Night Has a Thousand Eyes
2. SSA, piano
3. Frances W. Bourdillon
5. Schmidt, 1932
6. L of C

0496 No One Is Like Our God:
see Music for the Syna-
gogue.

0497 O Lord God, the Life of
Mortals: see Responses for
Church Use.

0498 O Zion That Bringest
Good Tidings
2. soli, SATB, organ
5. Schmidt, 1903, 1930
6. L of C

0499 The One Eternal God
2. SSAA, piano
3. Yigdal of Daniel Ben
    Judah
5. Schmidt, 1914, 1921
6. L of C

0500 Praise the Lord: see
Music for the Synagogue.

0501 Praised Be His Holy

Name: see Music for the
Synagogue.

0502 Recessional ("God of
Our Fathers"), 1915
2. TTBB, trumpet, 3
    trombones
3. Rudyard Kipling
5. Schmidt, 1914
6. L of C (vocal score);
    New England Cons. (brass
    parts)

0503 Response for the Third
Sabbath of the Month: see
Music for the Synagogue.

0504 Responses for Church
Use
2. SATB
3. biblical, except for
    when noted below
5. Schmidt, 1896, 1923-24
6. L of C
  a. Beloved, Let Us Love
      One Another
      (Horatius Bonar)
  b. The Beatitudes
  c. Search Me, O God
  d. O Lord God, the Life
      of Mortals
  e. I Will Arise and Go
      To My Father

0505 The Reveille, 1920
2. SATB
3. Bret Harte
5. Silver Burdett, 1920
6. unknown

0506 Sanctification: see
Music for the Synagogue.

0507 Scythe Song: see Four
Songs.

FOOTE

0508 Search Me, O God: see
Responses for Church Use.

0509 Seek and Ye Shall Find,
1915
2. TTBB, organ or piano
3. biblical
5. Schmidt, 1915
6. L of C

0510   same for SATB

0511 Sigh No More, Ladies
2. SSA, piano
3. Shakespeare
5. Schmidt, 1913
6. L of C

0512 The Skeleton in Armor,
Op. 28, 1891
2. SATB, orchestra
3. Henry W. Longfellow
4. 15 minutes
5. Schmidt, 1892, 1920
6. New England Cons.
(incomplete)

0513 The Skipper's Daughter:
see The Wreck of the Hes-
perus.

0514 Sleep, 1929
2. SSAA, piano
3. Thomas Bailey Aldrich
5. Schmidt, 1929, 1957
6. L of C

0515 A Song of April, 1905
2. S solo, TTBB, piano
3. E. M. M.

5. Schmidt, 1905, 1932;
Breitkopf, 1907
6. L of C

0516 Still, Still With Thee
2. SATB, organ
3. Harriet Beecher Stowe
5. Schmidt, 1893, 1920;
Curwen, 1904
6. L of C

0517 Te Deum in D
2. SATB, organ
3. liturgical
5. Schmidt, 1890, 1917
6. L of C

0518 Te Deum in B-flat,
1889
2. SATB, organ
3. liturgical
5. Schmidt, 1894, 1921
6. L of C

0519 Te Deum and Jubilate
in E-flat, Op. 7
2. SATB, organ
3. liturgical
5. Schmidt, 1886, 1913-14
6. Harvard Musical Assoc.
(personal copy of pub-
lished work)

0520 Thanks Be To God
2. SATB, organ
3. biblical
5. Schmidt, 1943
6. unknown

0521 Thine, O Lord, Is the
Greatness: see Music for
the Synagogue.

FOOTE

0522   Through the Rushes, by
the River
2. SSA, piano
3. Florence Earle Coates
5. Schmidt, 1913; Breitkopf,
1913
6. L of C

0523   Thy Way, Not Mine
2. ATB, organ
5. Schmidt, 1899, 1927
6. L of C
N.B.: later published in
four-part arrangement.

0524   To Daffodils, 1887
2. SSAA
3. Robert Herrick
5. Ditson, 1887
6. unknown

0525   Tomorrow
2. SSA, piano
3. Florence Earle Coates
5. Schmidt, 1911
6. L of C

0526   Too Soon, So Fair, Fair
Ladies: see Four Songs.

0527   The Trilliums: see
Flower Songs.

0528   Venite in C, 1889
2. SATB, organ
3. liturgical
5. Schmidt, 1892, 1920
6. L of C

0529   Vita nostra plena

bellis, Op. 47, 1900
2. SATB
3. Alanus Insulanus, trans.
John Lord Hayes
4. 18 minutes
5. Schmidt, 1901
6. L of C

0530   We Bend the Knee: see
Music for the Synagogue.

0531   Where Shall I Find a
White Rose Blowing?
2. SA, piano
3. Christina Rossetti
5. Schmidt, 1915
6. L of C

0532   Who Is Like Unto Thee:
see Music for the Syna-
gogue.

0533   The Wind and the Day:
see Four Songs.

0534   The Wreck of the
Hesperus: The Sailor's
Daughter, Op. 17, 1888
2. STB soli, SATB,
orchestra
3. Henry W. Longfellow
4. 25 minutes
5. Schmidt, 1888, 1915;
Curwen, 1889
6. L of C (full score,
incomplete vocal score)
7. 021, 100, 110

F R Y

0535   Crystal Palace Ode:
see Ode.

FRY

**0536 Each Merry Moss Trooper
Mounted His Steed**
2. TTBB, piano
6. Lib. Company of Phil.

0537 Hallelujah Chorus, n.d.
2. SATB, orchestra
3. biblical
4. 10 minutes
5. unpublished
6. Lib. Company of Phil.
7. 065

0538 Kyrie eleison, 1864?
2. SATB, orchestra
3. liturgical
5. unpublished
6. Lib. Company of Phil.
N.B.: orchestra parts missing

**0539 Laurels Twined Around
the Warrior's Brow**
2. SATB, piano
6. Lib. Company of Phil.

0540 The Lord God Omnipotent
2. SATB, orchestra, organ
5. unpublished
6. Lib. Company of Phil.
N.B.: incomplete

0541 Mass in E-flat, 1864
2. SATB, orchestra
3. liturgical
4. 15-20 minutes
5. unpublished
6. Lib. Company of Phil.
7. 065
N.B.: orchestrations
incomplete

0542 Moses in Egypt, n.d.

2. SATB soli, SATB,
orchestra
5. unpublished
6. Lib. Company of Phil.
N.B.: incomplete

0543 Ode, 1854
2. SATB, orchestra
4. 25 minutes
5. unpublished
6. Lib. Company of Phil.
7. 065

**0544 Stabat Mater, or The
Crucifixion of Christ,
1855**
2. SATB soli, SATB,
orchestra
3. liturgical
4. 60 minutes
5. Ditson, 1855
6. Lib. Company of Phil.
7. 065

G I L C H R I S T

**0545 Ah, Twinkling Star,
1903?**
2. SATB

**0546 Angels Roll the Stone
Away**, 1898
2. SSA
3. Thomas Scott
6. Free Lib. of Phil. (ms.
by copyist)

0547 Approach of Spring
2. SSAA
5. G. Schirmer, 1894

0548 Ave Maria, 1890
2. SATB/SATB, piano and

GILCHRIST

organ
5. publ. by author, Phila-
    delphia

0549 The Bells
2. SSAA, piano
3. Edgar Allen Poe
5. G. Schirmer, 1913

0550 Behold My Servant
2. TTBB, piano
3. biblical
5. G. Schirmer, 1894

0551 Behold Now, Fear Ye Not
2. S solo, SATB, organ
3. biblical
5. G. Schirmer, 1894

0552 Benedic anima in G
5. G. Schirmer, 1883

0553 Benedictus in F

0554 Benedictus in G

0555 Bethlehem
2. S solo, SATB, organ
3. Phillips Brooks
5. Church, 1898

0556 Bless the Lord, O My
    Soul
2. SATB, piano
3. biblical
6. Free Lib. of Phil.

0557 Bonum est

2. SATB
5. G. Schirmer

0558 Bugle Song
2. TTBB
3. Alfred Lord Tennyson
5. G. Schirmer, 1886
6. Free Lib. of Phil.

0559 Calm on the Listening
    Ear of Night
2. S solo, SATB, organ
3. Edmund Hamilton Sears
5. G. Schirmer, 1889

0560 Cantate Domino in G,
    No. 1
5. G. Schirmer, 1883

0561 Cantate Domino in G,
    No. 2

0562 Charm Me Asleep
2. SSA
3. Robert Herrick
5. Ditson, 1913

0563 Cherry Ripe
2. SSA
3. Robert Herrick
5. Ditson, 1913

0564 Christ Is Born the
    Angels Say
2. unison voices, piano
5. Ditson

0565 Christ is Risen
2. SATB, piano
3. biblical
5. Wm. H. Boner, 1877

GILCHRIST

0566 Christ Our Passover
2. SATB, organ
3. biblical
5. Wm H. Boner, 1879

0567 Christ Our Passover
3. biblical
5. G. Schirmer, 1883

0568 Christ Our Passover
2. SATB
3. biblical
5. G. Schirmer, 1887

0569 Christ the Lord Is
Risen Today
2. S solo, SATB, organ
3. Michael Weiss
5. G. Schirmer, 1886

0570 Christians Awake
2. SSAA, organ
5. G. Schirmer, 1886

0571 A Christmas Idyll, 1898
2. SATB soli, SATB,
orchestra
3. biblical
4. 45 minutes
5. Ditson, 1894

0572 Come Gracious Spirit
5. G. Schirmer

0573 Come O'er the Sea
2. Bar solo, SATB
5. G. Schirmer, 1886

0574 Come See the Place

Where Jesus Lay
2. S solo, SATB, piano
3. Richard Crashaw
5. publ. by author, 1887;
Church, 1895

0575 Come Shout Come Sing
of the Great Sea King
2. TTBB, piano
3. Barry Cornwall
6. Free Lib. of Phil.

0576 The Day Gently Sinking
2. Bar solo, SATB, piano
3. St. Anatolius
5. G. Schirmer, 1886

0577 The Day Is Past and
Over
2. solo, SATB, organ
3. St. Anatolius and J. M.
Neale
5. Ditson, 1914

0578 De profunsis (sic)
2. SATB, orchestra
3. biblical
6. Free Lib. of Phil.

0579 Dominus regit me
2. SAB
3. biblical
6. Free Lib. of Phil.

0580 Dreaming, Forever
Vainly Dreaming, 1880?
2. TTBB
3. Barry Cornwall
5. G. Schirmer, 1885

0581 Drinking Song
2. TTBB
3. Thomas Moore
5. G. Schirmer, 1886

GILCHRIST

0582 An Easter Idyll, 1907
2. SATB soli, SATB,
    orchestra, organ
3. biblical
5. G. Schirmer, 1907
6. Free Lib. of Phil.

0583 Emmanuel
2. SATB, organ
3. William C. Dix
5. Ditson, 1898

0584 Except the Lord Build
the House
2. SATB, organ
3. biblical
5. G. Schirmer, 1886

0585 Father Of All
2. SATB, piano or organ
3. John Julian

0586 The Fountain
2. SSAA, piano
3. James Russell Lowell
5. Presser, 1899

0587 The Future
2. SATB, piano
3. Sidney Lanier
5. H.W. Gray, 1908

0588 Gloria in excelsis in G
5. publ. by author, 1883

0589 Gloria in excelsis in C
5. G. Schirmer, 1889

0590 God Is My Strong
Salvation
2. T solo, SATB, organ
3. James Montgomery
5. G. Schirmer, 1905
6. L of C

0591 God Is Our Refuge and
Strength: see Psalm 46.

0592 God That Made Earth
and Heaven
2. S solo, SATB, organ
3. Reginald Heber
5. G. Schirmer, 1892

0593 Hark, What Mean Those
Holy Voices
2. S solo, SATB,organ
3. J. Carwood
5. G. Schirmer, 1895

0594 Hide Me O Twilight Air
2. SATB, piano four-hands
3. Barry Cornwall
5. G. Schirmer, 1910

0595 Home They Brought Her
Warrior Dead
2. ST, piano
3. Alfred Lord Tennyson
6. Free Lib. of Phil.

0596 How Long Wilt Thou
Forget Me, O Lord?
2. A solo, SATB, organ
3. biblical
6. Free Lib. of Phil.

0597 Hunting Song
2. SATB
3. Barry Cornwall
5. G. Schirmer, 1910

GILCHRIST

0598   I Heard the Voice of
Jesus Say
2.   T solo, SATB, organ
3.   Horatius Bonar
5.   G. Schirmer, 1909

0599   I Love My God
5.   Wm. H. Boner, 1883

0600   I Love Thee Lord
2.   S solo, SATB, keyboard
3.   Connie Calenberg
5.   E.S. Lorenz, 1900

0601   I Will Lift Up My Eyes
2.   SSA, piano
5.   G. Schirmer, 1889

0602   If Ye Then Be Rich with
Christ
2.   SATB, organ
3.   biblical
6.   Free Lib. of Phil.

0603   In Autumn, 1880
2.   TTBB
5.   G. Schirmer, 1885

0604   In the Blush of Evening
2.   S solo, SSAA
3.   Johann W. von Goethe
5.   Ditson, 1897

0605   It Came Upon a Midnight
Clear
2.   SATB, organ
3.   Edmund Hamilton Sears
5.   G. Schirmer, 1886

0606   Jesus, I My Cross Have
Taken, 1882
2.   SATB, organ
3.   Henry F. Lyle
5.   Ditson, 1905; Our
Sweetest Music, 1901
6.   L of C

0607   Jesus, Lover of My
Soul
2.   S solo, SATB, organ
3.   Charles Wesley
5.   G. Schirmer, 1903

0608   Jesus, the Very
Thought of Thee
2.   A solo, SATB, organ
3.   St. Bernard of Clairvaux
5.   G. Schirmer, 1892

0609   The Journey of Life
2.   TTBB
3.   William Cullan Bryant
5.   G. Schirmer, 1886

0610   Jubilate in C

0611   Jubilate in F

0612   Jubilate Deo in G
(copyright renewed in 1908)

0613   Jubilate Deo in A-flat
5.   G. Schirmer

0614   Jubilate Deo in B-flat
2.   SATB
5.   G. Schirmer, 1886

0615   Just As I Am, 1905
2.   soli, SATB, organ

GILCHRIST

5. G. Schirmer, 1905
6. L of C

**0616   The Knight of Tog-
genberg, 1878**
2. A solo, SSAA, piano
3. Friedrich von Schiller
4. 15 minutes
5. Ditson, 1911
6. Free Lib. of Phil.

0617   The Lamb of God, 1909
2. SATB soli, SATB,
narrator, organ
3. James Montgomery
4. 50-60 minutes
5. H.W. Gray, 1909

0618   Laudate
2. 8S 8A 8T 10B
6. Free Lib. of Phil.

**0619   The Legend of the
Bended Bow, 1888**
2. A solo, TTBB, piano
four-hands
3. Felicia Dorothea Browne
Hemans
4. 10 minutes
5. G. Schirmer, 1888

0620   The Lord Reigneth
2. SATB, keyboard
5. E. S. Lorenz, 1900

0621   Lord, What Is Man?
2. SATB
3. biblical
6. Free Lib. of Phil.

**0622   Lord, With a Glowing
Heart I'd Praise Thee**
5. Ditson, 1892

0623   Lullaby
2. SSAA
5. G. Schirmer

0624   Magnificat in F
5. publ. by author, 1887

**0625   Magnificat in G Major
(Festival)**
2. SATB, organ
5. G. Schirmer, 1887
6. Free Lib. of Phil.

0626   Merry Christmas
2. SSAATTBB
3. Margaret E. Sangster
5. Sliver Burdett, 1911

0627   Miranda
2. SATB
3. Sidney Lanier
5. H. W. Gray, 1908

0628   Morning Song
2. SSAA
5. G. Schirmer, 1894

0629   National Hymn, 1887
2. TTBB
3. F. Marion Crawford
5. W. H. Boner, 1887

0630   The Nights
2. SSA
3. Barry Cornwall
5. Ditson, 1897

GILCHRIST

0631 The Ninetieth Psalm
2. SATB, orchestra
3. biblical
4. 50 minutes
5. publ. by author, 1915
6. Free Lib. of Phil.

0632 No! No! It Is Not Dying
2. SATB
3. H.A.C. Malan
5. Charles S. Elliot and
Co., 1897

0633 No! Not Despairingly
2. SATB, organ
3. Horatius Bonar
5. Ditson, 1896

0634 Nunc dimittis in F
5. G. Schirmer

0635 O Captain! My Captain!
2. SATB, piano
3. Walt Whitman
6. Free Lib. of Phil.

0636 O Jesu, Thou Art Standing
2. A solo, SATB, organ
3. H. H. How
5. G. Schirmer, 1909

0637 O Lord the Proud Are Risen
2. SATB, organ
3. biblical
6. Free Lib. of Phil.

0638 O Many and Many a Year Ago

0639 O Saviour! Precious Saviour
2. S solo, SATB, organ
3. Francis Ridley Hauergal
6. Free Lib. of Phil.

0640 An Ode to the Sun, 1880
2. TTBB, piano four-hands
3. Francis Hemans
5. G. Schirmer, 1885

0641 Ponder My Words
2. S solo, SATB, organ
5. G. Schirmer, 1915

0642 Prayer and Praise, 1889
2. SATB soli, SATB, orchestra
3. anonymous
4. 40 minutes
5. G. Schirmer, 1888
6. L of C
7. 069

0643 Psalm 46, 1881
2. S solo, SATB, orchestra
3. biblical
4. 40 minutes
5. G. Schirmer, 1882
6. Free Lib. of Phil.
7. 102, 122

0644 Psalm 90: see The Ninetieth Psalm.

0645 Pyramus and Thisby

0646 Recessional
2. SATB, piano
3. Rudyard Kipling
4. 10 minutes
5. G. Schirmer, 1902

GILCHRIST

0647 Rolling On
2. SSAA, piano
3. Charles F. Cox
5. Schmidt, 1899

0648 The Rose, 1887
2. A solo, SATB, orchestra
3. James Russell Lowell
4. 15 minutes
5. G. Schirmer, 1887
6. Free Lib. of Phil.

0649 A Rose to a Rose
2. SATB
3. Sidney Lanier
5. H. W. Gray, 1908

0650 Saviour, Again to Thy Dear Name
5. G. Schirmer, 1889

0651 Saviour Like a Shepherd Lead Us, 1902?

0652 Saviour Whom I Fain Would Love
2. S solo, SATB, organ
3. Toplady
6. Free Lib. of Phil

0653 Sea Fairies
2. SSAA, piano four-hands
3. Alfred Lord Tennyson
5. G. Schirmer, 1879-80

0654 Shadows of the Evening Hours, 1905
2. A solo, SATB, organ
3. Adelaide A. Proctor
5. Ditson, 1905

0655 Shine! Shine!
2. SBar or ST
6. Free Lib. of Phil.

0656 Shout the Glad Tidings
2. SATB
3. W. A. Muhlenburg
5. G. Schirmer, 1887

0657 Sing, O Daughter of Zion, 1887

0658 Sing, O Sing, This Blessed Morn, 1905
2. S solo, SATB, organ
5. G. Schirmer, 1905

0659 Sing We Alleluia
2. SATB, organ
5. G. Schirmer, 1883

0660 Sinner Turn, Why Will Ye Die?
2. A solo, SATB, organ
3. Samuel Wesley
5. G. Schirmer, 1905

0661 Set Down, Sad Soul
2. SSA
3. Barry Cornwall
5. Ditson, 1897

0662 Sleep and Poetry
2. SSA
3. John Keats
6. Free Lib. of Phil.

0663 Softly the Echoes Come

0664 Spring Song
2. ATB
5. G. Schirmer, 1881

GILCHRIST

0665   same for TTBB
5. G. Schirmer, 1886

0666   A Summer's Day: see
  Three Summer Songs.

0667   A Summer's Morn: see
  Three Summer Songs.

0668   A Summer's Night: see
  Three Summer Songs.

0669   Sweet Saviour, Bless Us
  Ere We Go
2. SATB, organ
3. Frederick W. Faber
5. G. Schirmer, 1887

0670   The Syrens, 1904
2. SSAA, flute, horn,
  violin, cello, piano
3. James Russell Lowell
4. 15 minutes
5. G. Schirmer, 1904

0671   Te Deum in C
3. liturgical
5. publ. by author, 1886

0672   Te Deum in F, No. 1
3. liturgical
5. publ. by author, 1883

0673   Te Deum in F, No. 2
3. liturgical
5. G. Schirmer

0674   Te Deum in G, No. 1

0675   Te Deum in G, No. 2
3. liturgical
5. publ. by author, 1883

0676   Te Deum in A-flat
3. liturgical
5. G. Schirmer

0677   Te Deum in A
  (Festival)
3. liturgical

0678   Te Deum in B-flat,
  1886
3. liturgical

0679   Te Dominum in F
2. SATB, organ
3. liturgical
5. G. Schirmer, 1882

0680   Three Summer Songs
2. SSA
3. Walt Whitman and Celia
  Thaxter
5. Ditson, 1914
  a. A Summer's Morn
  b. A Summer's Day
  c. A Summer's Night

0681   To Song, 1907?
2. SATB, piano
3. Gilchrist
5. publ. by author
7. 102

0682   The Uplifted Gates
2. SATB, piano four-hands
5. G. Schirmer, 1884

0683   Weary of Earth
2. S solo, SATB, organ
3. S. J. Stone
5. Ditson, 1898

GILCHRIST

0684 What E'er My God
Ordains Is Right
2. A solo, SATB, keyboard
3. S. Rodigast, trans.
Catherine Winkworth
5. H.W. Gray, 1914

0685 What is More Gentle
2. SSA, piano
3. John Keats
5. Ditson, 1906
6. Free Lib. of Phil.
(incomplete)

0686 When the Weary Seeking
Rest, 1904
2. SATB, keyboard
3. Horatius Bonar
5. Geibel and Lehman, 1904

0687 Ye Mountains Falls On
Us (sic)

G R I F F E S

0688 Dies ist der Tag, 1906
2. SSATB
3. Isaac Watts
5. unpublished
6. New York Public Lib.

0689 Lobe den Herrn, 1906
2. SSATB
3. Joachim Neander
5. unpublished
6. New York Public Lib.

0690 O Haupt voll Blut,
1906
2. SSATB
3. P. Gerhardt
5. unpublished
6. New York Public Lib.

0691 These Things Shall Be,
1916
2. unison voices, piano
3. John Addington Symonds
5. G. Schirmer, 1917
6. unknown

H A D L E Y

0692 The Admiral of the
Seas
2. T solo, SATB, orchestra
3. Cordelia Brooks Fenno
4. 20 minutes
5. C.C. Birchard, 1928

0693 Agnus Dei, 1919
2. A solo, SATB, orchestra
3. liturgical
4. 10 minutes
6. New York Public Lib.

0694 Amen, 19?
2. SATB
6. New York Public Lib.

0695 America to France
2. SATB, orchestra
3. Louise Ayres Garnett
5. Edition Salabert, 1919

HADLEY

0696 Autumn Song
2. SSAA, piano
3. Edmund Clarence Stedman
5. C. Fischer, 1933

0697 Ballad of June
2. TTBB, piano
3. W. E. Henley
5. Schmidt, 1901

0698 A Ballade of Mid-Summer
2. TTBB
3. Clinton Scollard
5. Schmidt, 1898

0699 Belshazzar, Op. 112, 1932
2. SATB soli, SATB, orchestra
3. Louise Ayres Garnett
4. 25 minutes
5. Presser, 1932
6. L of C (photocopy)

0700 Benedictus: see Church Service in E-flat.

0701 Bid Me to Live
2. SSAA, piano
3. Robert Herrick
5. G. Ricordi (N.Y.), 1930

0702 Blessed are the Undefiled: see Two Anthems.

0703 The Catechist, Op. 51, No. 2
2. SSA
5. G. Schirmer, 1911

0704 The Cautious Cat
2. TTBB
3. David Stevens
5. C.C. Birchard, 1916

0705 Chorus for Spanish Dance, 192?
2. SATB
6. New York Public Lib.

0706 Christ Our Passover, 1894?
2. SATB, organ
3. biblical
4. 12 minutes
5. Boston Music Co., 1894

0707 Christ Our Passover: see Easter Anthem.

0708 Christmas Carol, 1917
2. SATB
3. Gilbert K. Chesterton
6. New York Public Lib.

0709 Church Service in E-flat, Op. 56
2. SATB, organ
3. liturgical
5. H. W. Gray
6. New York Public Lib.
   a. Te Deum
   b. Jubilate Deo
   c. Benedictus
   d. Holy Communion
   e. Magnificat and Nunc dimittis
N.B.: Magnificat exists in two keys: E-flat and, later, C.

0710 Dearest, When I Am Dead: see Four Partsongs.

HADLEY

0711   Dedication Ode
2.   SSAA, piano
3.   Henry Van Dyke
4.   10 minutes
5.   Galaxy Music

0712   same for TTBB
5.   G. Ricordi, 1930

0713   Divine Tragedy, Op. 139
2.   SATB soli, SATB,
      orchestra
5.   unpublished

0714   Easter Anthem: Christ
Our Passover, 19?
2.   SATB soli, SATB,
      orchestra
3.   biblical
4.   10 minutes
5.   Boston Music Co., 1894
6.   New York Public Lib.

0715   Easter Cantata: see
Divine Tragedy.

0716   Even Song
2.   TTBB
3.   Sir Edward Bulwer Lytton
5.   Schmidt, 1898

0717   The Fairies, Op. 3,
1894
2.   S solo, SATB, orchestra
3.   William Allingham
4.   12 minutes
5.   Boston Music Co., 1894

0718   The Fairy Thorn, Op. 76
2.   SA soli, SSA, orchestra

3.   Cordelia Brooks Fenno
4.   15 minutes
5.   G. Schirmer, 1917

0719   The Fairy Wedding, Op.
106, 1931
2.   SA, piano
3.   Louise Ayres Garnett
4.   15 minutes
5.   C.C. Birchard, 1931

0720   The Fate of Princess
Kiyo: A Legend of Japan,
Op. 58, 1907
2.   S solo, SSAA, orchestra
3.   Edward Oxenford
4.   35 minutes
5.   G. Schirmer, 1907

0721   The Flag
2.   SATB, piano
3.   Joel Lewis
5.   C.C. Birchard

0722   The Fountain
2.   SATB, piano
3.   James Russell Lowell
5.   C. C. Birchard

0723   Four Partsongs, Op.
125
2.   SATB, piano
3.   Shakespeare, et al.
5   Presser, 1932
     a.   It Was a Bowl of
          Roses
     b.   Dearest, When I Am
          Dead
     c.   June and a Warm
          Sweet Rain
     d.   It Was a Lover and
          His Lass

HADLEY

0724 Gettysburg Address
2. solo, SATB, piano
3. Abraham Lincoln
5. C.C. Birchard, 1941

0725 The Golden Prince, Op.
69 (70?), 1914
2. SBar soli, SSAA,
orchestra
3. David Stevens (adapted
from Oscar Wilde)
4. 20 minutes
5. G. Schirmer, 1914
6. L of C

0726 Good Night, Op. 1, No.
3
2. TTBB
3. Amélie Rives
5. Boston Music Co., 1894
6. L of C (composer's
autographed printed copy)

0727 Gypsies
2. TTBB
3. Rachel Lyman Field
5. C. Fischer, 1934

**0728 He that Dwelleth in the
Secret Place**
2. B solo, SATB, organ
3. biblical
5. G. Schirmer, 1907

0729 Hoist the Flag
2. TTBB
3. Phyllis Lintott
5. G. Schirmer

0730 Holy Communion: see
Church Service in E-flat.

0731 A Hong Kong Romance
2. SATB, piano
5. Schmidt, 1903, 1908

0732 same for SSA
5. Schmidt, 1903, 1908

0733 same for TTBB
5. Schmidt, 1904

0734 How it Happened
2. SSAA, piano
3. Marco Fuller
5. Schmidt, 1903

**0735 How Silent, How
Spacious**
2. SATB, piano or organ
3. Ralph Waldo Emerson
5. Schmidt, 1904

0736 same for SSAA
5. Schmidt, 1931

0737 The Immortal
2. SATB, piano
3. Cale Young Rice
5. A Book of Choruses,
Silver Burdett, 1923

0738 In Arcady, Op. 83
2. SATB, orchestra
5. unpublished

0739 In Music's Praise, Op.
21, 1899
2. SATB soli, SATB,
orchestra
3. G.F.R. Anderson
4. 35 minutes
5. Ditson, 1900; Lyon and
Healy, 1900

HADLEY

0740 It Was a Bowl of Roses:
see Four Partsongs.

0741 It Was a Lover and His
Lass: see Four Part Songs.

0742 It Was Not in the
Winter: see Partsongs.

0743 Jabberwocky
2. SATB, orchestra
5. unpublished

0744 The Joyful Morn, 19?
2. SATB, organ
6. New York Public Lib.
N.B.: A note in the NYPL
questions Hadley's author-
ship of this work.

0745 Jubilate Deo: see
Church Service in E-flat.

0746 Jubilate Deo
2. unison voices
3. liturgical
5. Novello, 1901

0747 June and a Warm Sweet
Rain: see Four Partsongs.

0748 A Legend of Granada,
Op. 45, 1904
2. SBar soli, SSAA,
orchestra
3. Ethel Watts Mumford
4. 30 minutes
5. G. Schirmer, 1904

0749 A Legend of Niagara:
see Lelawala.

0750 Lelawala: A Legend of
Niagara, Op. 13, 1898
2. ST soli, SATB, orchestra
3. G.F.R. Anderson
4. 20 minutes
5. Schmidt, 1898
7. 021

0751 The Lord is My
Strength and Song
2. AB soli, SATB, organ
5. G. Schirmer, 1908

0752 The Lucky Horseshoe
2. TTBB
3. David Stevens
5. G. Schirmer, 1916

0753 Magnificat and Nunc
dimittis: see Church
Service in E-flat.

0754 May Day
2. SATB, orchestra
3. A. L. Jansson
5. Boston Music Co., 1894

0755 Merlin and Vivian, Op.
52, 190??
2. SATB soli, SATB,
orchestra
3. Ethel Watts Mumford
4. 60 minutes
5. G. Schirmer, 1907

0756 Mirtil in Arcadia, Op.
100, 1926
2. STB soli, SATB,
children, narrator, or-
chestra
3. Louise Ayres Garnett

HADLEY

4. 90 minutes
5. C.C. Birchard, 1927,
   1928

0757 **Music: An Ode**, Op. 75,
   1917?
2. SATB soli, SATB,
   orchestra
3. Henry Van Dyke
4. 90 minutes
5. G. Schirmer, 1917
6. New York Public Lib.
   (autograph); L of C
   (incomplete holograph)

0758 **The Musical Trust**
2. TTBB
3. David Stevens
5. G. Schirmer, 1914

0759 **My Shadow**, Op. 29
2. SSA, piano
3. Robert Louis Stevenson
5. Schmidt, 1893, 1909

0760 same for SATB
5. Schmidt, 1903, 1909

0761 same for TTBB,
5. Schmidt, 1930

0762 **The New Earth**, Op. 85,
   1919?
2. SATB soli, SATB,
   orchestra
3. Louise Ayres Garnett
4. 60 minutes
5. Ditson, 1919

0763 **Night**

2. TTBB
3. Katherine Washburn
   Harding
5. R.D. Row, 1938

0764 **The Nightingale and
   the Rose**, Op. 54, 1911?
2. S solo, SSAA, orchestra
3. Ethel Watts Mumford
4. 20 minutes
5. G. Schirmer, 1911;
   Schmidt

0765 **O Lady Mine**
2. SATB
3. Clinton Scollard
5. Schmidt, 1897

0766 **Ode to Music**: see
   Music: An Ode.

0767 **Orchards**
2. SSA, piano
3. Clara Edwards
5. C. Fischer, 1933

0768 **Out of the Depths**:
   see **Two Anthems**.

0769 **Partsongs**, Op. 81
2. TTBB
3. see below
5. G. Schirmer, 1921
6. New York Public Lib.
   a. The Passing of
      Spring (Lillian P.
      Wilson)
   b. Sabbath Day (Maybel
      Hayden), 1891
   c. It Was Not in the
      Winter (Thomas
      Hood), 1827

HADLEY

0770   The Passing of Spring:
see Partsongs.

0771   The Pixies, Op. 1, No.
   1
2.   TTBB
3.   Samuel M. Peck
5.   Boston Music Co., 1894

0772   The Postilion's Song
2.   SATB
3.   David Stevens
5.   Silver Burdett, 1915

0773   The Princess of Ys, Op.
   34, 1903
2.   SSAA, piano
3.   Ethel Watts Mumford
4.   12 minutes
5.   Schmidt, 1903
6.   New York Public Lib.; L
   of C (undated autograph
   score)

0774   same for SATB
5.   Schmidt, 1934

0775   Prophecy and Ful-
   fillment, Op. 91, 1922?
2.   SAT soli, SATB, 3 horns,
   3 trumpets, 3 trombones,
   timp.
3.   biblical
4.   25 minutes
5.   H. Flammer
   a.   Chorus and Fugue
   b.   Of the Father's Love
      Begotten
   c.   While Shepherds
      Watched Their Flocks
   d.   When From the East
      the Wise Men Came
   e.   Hush My Dear, Lie
      Still and Slumber
   f.   Glory Be to God
      Almighty

0776   Recessional, Op. 38,
   No. 1
2.   SATB, organ
3.   Rudyard Kipling
5.   Schmidt, 1904

0777   Resurgam, Op. 98,
   1922?
2.   soli, SATB, orchestra
3.   Louise Ayres Garnett
4.   70 minutes
5.   Ditson, 1922
6.   New York Public Lib.
   (two composer's cor-
   rected scores)

0778   Roads
2.   TTBB
3.   Rachel Lyman Field
5.   Galaxy Music, 1937

0779   same for SSA
5.   C. Fisher, 1934

0780   Sabbath Day: see
   Partsongs.

0781   Sanctus, 19?
2.   S solo, SSAA, orchestra
3.   liturgical
6.   New York Public Lib.

0782   Sea Fever
2.   SATB, piano
3.   John Masefield
5.   A Book of Choruses,
   Silver Burdett, 1923

HADLEY

0783 Semper vivrens, Op. 97
2. soli, SATB, orchestra
5. C. Fischer

0784 A Snowflake
2. SSA, piano
3. Clinton Scollard
5. Schmidt, 1930

0785 Song of the Sea, Op.
117, No. 1
2. TTBB
3. Allan Cunningham
5. Hill-Coleman, 1936

0786 Te Deum: see Church
Service in E-flat.

0787 There Was a Little Man
2. SATB, piano
3. Frederick Manley
5. Schmidt, 1904

0788 There Were Shepherds,
Op. 11
2. SATb, piano or organ
5. Schmidt

0789 Three Poems by
Shakespeare, Op. 81
2. SATB
3. Shakespeare
5. G. Schirmer, 1918
   a. Love
   b. For Bonnie Sweet Rain
   c. O Mistress Mine

0790 Thrushes
2. SATB
3. Rachel Lyman Field

5. C. Fischer, 1934

0791 The Time of Parting,
Op. 84, No. 2
2. SSA, piano
3. Rabindranath Tagore
5. C. Fischer, 1925

0792 The Toll of the Sea,
Op. 67, No. 1
2. SSA
3. David Stevens
4. 12 minutes
5. G. Schirmer, 1913

0793 Two Anthems, Op. 71
2. SATB, piano
3. biblical
4. 12 minutes (both)
5. Ditson; G. Schirmer,
1918
   a. Out of the Depths
   b. Blessed are the Un-
defiled

0794 The Walrus and the
Carpenter
2. TTBB
3. Lewis Carroll
5. G. Schirmer, 1904

0795 The Water Lily, Op. 1,
No. 2
2. TTBB
3. Heinrich Heine
5. Boston Music Co., 1894

0796 What the Winds Bring
2. SSAA, piano
3. Edmund Clarence Stedman
5. C. Fischer, 1933

H E I N R I C H

0797   The Adieu, 1845
2. SATBB soli, SATBB,
    orchestra
3. Charles J. Hempel, trans.
    William J. Edson
4. 20 minutes
5. publ. by author, 1845

0798   Adoramus te, Christe:
see Musings of the Wild
Wood.

0799   Amor Patriae: see
Musings of the Wild Wood.

0800   A Bottle Song
2. STB, piano
3. Robert Burns

0801   The City of Fraternal
Love: see The Tribute:
The City of Fraternal Love.

0802   The Columbiad, 1857-58
2. SATBB soli, SATB/SATB,
    orchestra
3. Dr. Langenschwartz
4. 25 minutes
6. L of C
7. 038
    a. Soli Deo gloria
    b. Erkenne Gott

0803   Coro funerale (Funeral
Anthem), 1847
2. SATBB soli, SATB, semi-
    chorus, orchestra, organ
3. Mary E. Hewitt
5. C. Holt, Jr., 1847
6. L of C

0804   The Dawning of Music
in Kentucky; or, The Pleasures of Harmony in the
Solitude of Nature, Op. 1;
bound together with The
Western Minstrel, Op. 2
2. SATB
5. Bacon and Hart, 1820;
    Da Capo, 1972
6. L of C
7. 038, 124

0805   The Death of a Christian: see Musings of the
Wild Wood.

0806   Elegiac quintetto
vocale, 1846
2. SATBB , organ, piano
3. William Wallace
4. 10 minutes
5. C.G. Christman, 1846

0807   Epitaph on Joan Bugg,
1825
2. SAATB (or SATTB), piano
3. William Staunton

0808   Erkenne Gott!:   see
The Columbiad.

0810   Farewell to My Log
House: see Sequel.

0811   Die Felsen von
Plymouth, 1858-59
2. soli, SATB, orchestra
6. L of C

0812   Fill Your Goblets,
1825
2. SATB, piano

HEINRICH

0813 Funeral Anthem, 1832
2. 2 treble, TBB soli, SATB,
    organ or piano
3. Charles Murray
5. C. Bradlee, 183?

0814 Funeral Anthem, 1847:
see Coro funerale.

0815 The Great Republic, An
Ode to the American Union,
Op. 47
3. William Oland Bourne

0816 Hail Beauteous Spring
2. SSB, piano
3. W. B. Tappan
5. C. Bradlee, 1832

0817 The Jubilee, 1841
2. SATBB soli, SATBB,
    orchestra
3. William J. Edson
6. L of C
7. 038

0818 The Minstrel's Adieu,
1826
2. SSB, piano
3. C. H. Locke

0819 The Minstrel's Catch:
see The Sylviad.

0820 Minstrelsy of Nature in
the Wilds of North America:
see The Sylviad.

0821 Music, the Harmonizer

of the World, 1851
2. solo, SATB, piano

0822 Musings of the Wild
Wood, 1836-54
2. (varies:) SATB soli,
    SATB, orchestra
3. see below
6. L of C
    a. Noble Emperor, Thine
        the Glory (William
        Jarvis Wetmore)
    b. Amor Patriae
        (Wetmore)
    c. The Warrior's March
        to the Battlefield
        (Wetmore)
    d. Missa sacra, No. 2:
        Adoramus te, Christe
    e. Missa sacra, No. 3:
        O sancta Maria
    f. Missa sacra, No. 4:
        The Death of a
        Christian (August
        Mandel)

0823 Niagara, Op. 62
2. soli, SATB, orchestra

0824 O sancta Maria: see
Musings of the Wild Wood.

0825 O santa Maria (sic),
1834
2. 14 parts, concertante;
    choral/orchestral
3. W. Steele
6. L of C

0826 Ode by Collins: How
Sleep the Brave, 1818
2. STB, piano
3. Collins

HEINRICH

0827 Our Hearts Are with Our
      Native Land, 1851?
2. SATBB, piano

0828 Philanthropy
2. SATBB, piano
3. Heinrich

0829 The Pilgrims to the New
      World: see The Wild Wood
      Spirit's Chant.

0830 The Pleasures of Har-
      mony in the Solitude of
      Nature: see The Dawning of
      Music in Kentucky.

0831 Soli Deo gloria: see
      The Columbiad.

0832 The Sylviad; or, Min-
      strelsy of Nature in the
      Wilds of North America, Op.
      3, 1823, 1825-26
2. SATB, orchestra
5. Gaupner, 1825
7. 038

0833 The Tribute: The City
      of Fraternal Love, 1846
2. solo, SATB, piano

0834 The Western Minstrel:
      Op. 2: see The Dawning of
      Music in Kentucky

0835 The Western Minstrel's
      Musical Compliments to Mrs.
      Coutts

2. SSB, piano
3. Heinrich (?)

0836 The Warrior's March to
      the Battlefield: see
      Musings of the Wild Wood.

0837 The Wild Wood Spirit's
      Chant; or, The Pilgrims to
      the New World, 1845
3. William J. Edson
5. publ. by author, 1845
6. L of C
    a. The Adieu
    b. Jubilee

I V E S

0838 The Bells of Yale; or,
      Chapel Chimes, 1897-98
2. Bar solo, TTBB, piano
3. Huntington Mason
5. Yale Melodies, 1903
6. Yale

0839 Benedictus in E, 1890?
2. SATB, organ
3. biblical
6. Yale

0840 Benedictus in G, 1891
2. SATB
3. biblical
6. Yale (fragment)

0841 Bread of the World,
      1891?
2. unison female voices,
    organ
3. Reginald Heber
6. Yale

IVES

0842   The Celestial Country,
   1898
2.   SSAATTBB soli, SATB,
   strings, trumpet, eupho-
   nium, timp., organ
3.   Henry Alford
4.   20 minutes
5.   Peer, 1971, 1973
6.   Yale
7.   011, 049, 061, 111, 114,
   129, 131
   a.   Far O'er Yon Horizon:
      Prelude, Trio and
      Chorus
   b.   Naught that Country
      Needeth
   c.   Seek the Things
      before Us
   d.   Intermezzo
   e.   Glories on Glories
   f.   Forward, Flock of
      Jesus
   g.   To the Eternal
      Father: Chorale and
      Prelude

0843   Chapel Chimes: see The
   Bells of Yale.

0844   Circus Band, 1894
2.   SSAATTBB, orchestra
5.   Peer, 1969, 1971

0845   Communion Service, 1891
2.   SATB, organ
3.   liturgical/biblical
6.   Yale

0846   Crossing the Bar, 1890?
2.   SATB, organ
3.   Alfred Lord Tennyson
5.   Assoc. Music Publ., 1974
6.   Yale

0847   December, 1912-3
2.   unison men's voices,
   piccolo, 2 clarinets, 2
   horns, 3 trumpets, 3
   trombones, tuba
3.   Dante G. Rossetti, after
   Folgore
5.   Peer, 1963
6.   Yale

0848   Easter Carol, 1892
2.   SATB soli, SATB, organ
3.   unknown
4.   10 minutes
5.   Assoc. Music Publ., 1923
6.   Yale

0849   An Election, 1920
2.   unison voices, orchestra
3.   Ives
6.   Yale
N.B.: also titled: "Down
with Politicians"

0850   Experimental Canticle
   Phrases, 1891-92
2.   SATB
6.   Yale

0851   For You and Me!, 1895-
   96
2.   TTBB
3.   Ives?
5.   G. Molineaux, 1896
   (Molineaux' Collection
   of Partsongs and Chor-
   uses for Male Voices);
   J. Boonin, 1973
6.   Yale

0852   General Booth, 1914
2.   unison voices, band
3.   N. Vachel Lindsay
5.   Presser, n.d.; Merion
   Music, 1964

IVES

6. Yale

0853 Glories on Glories: see
Celestial Country.

0854 God of My Life, 1892?
2. SATB, organ
3. Charlotte Elliott
6. Yale

0855 Harvest Home: see
Three Harvest Home Cho-
rales.

0856 Harvest Home Chorales:
see Three Harvest Home
Chorales.

0857 He Is There!, 1917
2. unison voices, orchestra
3. Ives
6. Yale

0858 Hymn, Op. 2, No. 1,
1887
2. SATB
3. textless
6. Yale

0859 I Think of Thee, My
God, 1889?
2. SATB
3. John S. B. Monsell
6. Yale

0860 Johnny Poe, 1925
2. TTBB, orchestra
3. Benjamin R. C. Low
6. Yale (fragment)

0861 Let There Be Light:
see Processional.

0862 The Light that is
Felt, 1895?
2. solo, SATB, organ
3. John Greenleaf Whittier
6. Yale

0863 Lincoln, the Great
Commoner, 1912
2. unison voices, orchestra
3. Edwin Markham
5. New Music (New York),
1976
6. Yale

0864 Lord God, Thy Sea Is
Mighty, 1893?
2. SATB, organ
6. Yale

0865 Lord of the Harvest:
see Three Harvest Home
Chorales.

0866 Majority (The Masses),
1914-15
2. unison voices, orchestra
3. Ives
6. Yale

0867 The Masses: see The
Majority.

0868 'Neath the Elm Trees,
1895?
2. TTBB
6. Yale

0869 The New River, 1910
2. two-part choir,

IVES

orchestra
3. Ives
5. Peer, 1970, 1971
6. Yale
7. 129

0870 O Maiden Fair, 1898-99
2. Bar solo, TTBB, piano
6. Yale

0871 Processional: Let
There Be Light, 1901
2. TTBB or SATB, organ or
strings, brass
3. John Ellerton
5. Peer, 1967, 1955
6. Yale
7. 133

0872 Psalm 14, 1899?
2. SATB/SATB, organ
3. biblical
5. Mercury, 195?
6. Yale
7. 111

0873 Psalm 24, 1897
2. SSAATTBB
3. biblical
5. Mercury, 1955
6. Yale
7. 003, 119, 131, 132

0874 Psalm 25, 1899-1901?
2. SSAATTBB, organ
3. biblical
5. Merion, 1979
6. Yale
7. 131

0875 Psalm 42, 1888?
2. SATB, organ
3. biblical
6. Yale

0876 Psalm 54, 1894?
2. SAATBB
3. biblical
4. 10 minutes
5. Merion, 1973; Mercury,
195?
6. Yale
7. 114

0877 Psalm 67, 1894?
2. SSAATTBB
3. biblical
5. Arrow Music Press, 1939
6. Yale
7. 061, 111, 114, 131, 132

0878 Psalm 90, 1894-1924
2. SSAATTBB, bells, organ
3. biblical
4. 10 minutes
5. Merion Music, 1970
6. Yale
7. 006, 037, 043, 111, 131

0879 Psalm 100, 1898-99?
2. SSAATTBB, SSAA, bells ad
lib.
3. biblical
4. 10 minutes
5. Merion Music, 1966, 1975
6. Yale
7. 111

0880 Psalm 135, 1900?
2. SSAATTBB, timp., organ,
brass, tenor/bass drum
3. biblical
5. Merion Music, 1981
6. Yale
7. 135

0881 Psalm 139: see Search
Me , O Lord.

0882 Psalm 150, 1894?
2. SSAATTBB, SSAA, organ
3. biblical
5. Presser, 1972
6. Yale
7. 111

IVES

0883 Search Me, O Lord,
  1891-92
2. SATB
3. biblical
6. Yale

0884 Serenade, 1891?
2. SATB
3. Henry W. Longfellow
6. Yale

0885 Serenity, 1909?
2. unison voices, piano
3. John Greenleaf Whittier
5. Assoc. Music Publ., 1942;
    Arrow Music Press, 1942
7. 045

0886 Sneak Thief, 1914
2. unison voices, trumpet,
    piano four-hands
3. Ives
6. Yale

0887 A Song of Mary's, 1896
2. TTBB
3. Charles Edmund Merrill,
    Jr.
5. Yale Courant, 33/9. 1897
6. Yale

0888 They Are There!, 1942
2. unison voices, orchestra
3. Ives
5. Peer, 1956, 1961, 1976
6. Yale

**0889 Three Harvest Home
  Chorales**, 1898-1901
2. SATTB, trumpets,
    trombone, tuba, organ
3. see below

4. 20 minutes
5. Mercury, 1949
6. Yale
7. 001, 046, 071, 119, 131,
    132
    a. Harvest Home (George
        Burgess)
    b. Lord of the Harvest
        (John Hempton
        Gurney)
    c. Harvest Home (Henry
        Alford)

0890 Turn Ye, Turn Ye,
  1890?
2. SATB, organ or piano
3. Josiah Hopkins
5. Presser, 1955, 1973
6. Yale

0891 Walt Whitman, 1913
2. unison voices, orchestra
3. Walt Whitman
6. Yale

**0892 The Year's at the
  Spring**, 1889?
2. SATB
3. Robert Browning
6. Yale

L O E F F L E R

0893 L'Archet, Op. 26, 1901
2. S solo, SSAA, viola
    d'amore, piano
5. C. C. Birchard
6. L of C

0894 Ave maris stella
2. S solo, unison boys or
    women, strings, piano,

LOEFFLER

organ
3. biblical/liturgical
6. L of C

0895   Beat! Beat! Drums!,
    1917
2. unison male voices,
    winds, drums, 2 pianos
3. Walt Whitman
4. 10 minutes
5. C. C. Birchard, 1932
6. L of C

0896   By the Rivers of
    Babylon, Op. 3, 1907
2. SSAA, cello, 2 flutes,
    organ, harp
3. biblical
4. 10 minutes
5. G. Schirmer, 1907

0897   Canticum fratris solis,
    1929
2. SSA
3. St. Francis of Assisi
4. 12 minutes
6. L of C
7. 108

0898   Drei Marienlieder für
gemischten Chor
2. SSAATTBB
3. biblical
6. L of C ("Angelus" only)
    a. Angelus Domini nun
        tiavit Mariae
    b. Remember, O Most
        Pious Virgin, Mary
    c. The Litany of the
        Blessed Virgin

0899   Evocation, 1931
2. SSAA, orchestra

3. Greek, trans. J. W.
    Machail
4. 10 minutes
5. Birchard and Co., 1932
6. L of C

0900   For One Who Fell in
    Battle, 1911
2. SSAATTBB
3. T. W. Parsons
4. 12 minutes
5. G. Schirmer, 1911

0901   Hora mystica, 1916
2. male voices, orchestra
4. 40 minutes
6. L of C

0902   Psalm 137: see By the
Rivers of Babylon.

0903   The Sermon on the
    Mount
2. SSAA, 2 viola d'amore,
    viola da gamba, harp,
    organ
3. biblical
6. L of C

M A C D O W E L L

0904   Alma mater, 1907?
2. female voices
4. Schmidt, 1907

0905   As the Gloaming Sha-
    dows Creep: see Two Songs
    from the Thirteenth Cen-
    tury.

MACDOWELL

0906   At Parting
2. female voices
3. MacDowell
5. Schmidt, 1907

**0907   A Ballad of Charles the
Bold**, Op. 54, No. 1, 1897
2. male voices
3. MacDowell
5. P.L. Jung, 1898; Schmidt
6. L of C

0908   Barcarolle, Op. 44,
1890
2. SSAATTBB, piano four-
hands
3. F. von Bodenstedt
5. Schmidt, 1892
6. L of C
7. 100

0909   Bonnie Ann, Op. 53, No.
1, 1896-97
2. TTBB
3. Robert Burns
5. P.L. Jung, 1898; Schmidt
6. L of C

0910   The Brook: see **Two
Northern Songs**.

0911   College Songs, 1900-01
2. TTBB
3. see below
5. Schmidt, 1901-02
6. L of C (b only)
    a. Columbia's Sons (E.
        Keppler)
    b. We Love Thee Well,
        Manhattanland
        (MacDowell)
    c. Columbia! O Alma
        mater (MacDowell)

d. Sturdy and Strong
    (MacDowell)
e. O Wise Old Alma
    mater (MacDowell)
f. At Parting
    (MacDowell)

0912   The Collier Lassie,
Op. 53, No. 2, 1896-97
2. TTBB
3. Robert Burns
5. P.L. Jung, 1898; Schmidt

**0913   Columbia! O Alma ma-
ter**: see **College Songs**.

0914   Columbia's Sons: see
College Songs.

0915   Cradle Song, Op. 41,
No. 1, 1890
2. SSAA
3. after P. Cornelius
5. Schmidt, 1890, 1915

0916   same for TTBB
5. Schmidt, 1907

0917   The Crusaders, Op. 52,
No. 3, 1896-97
2. TTBB
3. MacDowell
5. P.L.Jung, 1897; Schmidt

0918   Dance of Gnomes, Op.
41, No. 2, 1890
2. TTBB
3. MacDowell
5. Schmidt, 1890, 1907

0919   same for SSAA
5. Schmidt, 1916

MACDOWELL

0920 Drei Lieder für Männerchor, Op. 27, 1887
2. TTBB
3. see below; English texts
by MacDowell
5. Schmidt, 1890
6. Columbia University
7. 091
a. Oben wo die Sterne
glühen (Heinrich
Heine)
b. Schweizerlied
(Goethe)
c. Der Fischerknabe
(Frederich von
Schiller)

0921 Der Fischerknabe: see
Drei Lieder für vier-
stimmigen Männerchor.

0922 Eldorado, Op. 39
2. TTBB
3. Edgar Allen Poe
6. L of C

0923 From the Sea, Op. 52,
No. 2, 1896-97
2. TTBB
3. MacDowell
5. P.L. Jung, 1897; Schmidt,
1897
6. Columbia University

0924 same for SSAA
5. Schmidt, 1897

0925 Hush, Hush, Op. 52, No.
1, 1896-97
2. TTBB
3. Thomas Moore
5. P.L. Jung, 1897; Schmidt

0926 Hymn of the Pilgrim,
Op. 55, No. 3
2. SATB, piano
3. Hermann Hagedorn
5. Schmidt, 1920

0927 same for SSAA
5. Schmidt

0928 same for TTBB
5. Schmidt

0929 In the Starry Sky
Above Us: see Drei Lieder
für vierstimmigen Männer-
chor ("Oben wo die Sterne
glühen").

0930 Love and Time, Op. 3,
No. 1, 1896
2. TTBB
3. Marion Farley
5. P.L. Jung, 1897;
Schmidt
N.B.: written under pseud.
Edgar Thorn(e).

0931 Midsummer Clouds, Op.
54, No. 2, 1887
2. TTBB
3. MacDowell
5. P.L. Jung, 1898;
Schmidt

0932 same for SSAA
5. Schmidt, 1898, 1899,
1916

0933 O Wise Old Alma mater:
see College Songs.

MACDOWELL

0934 Oben wo die Sterne
glühen: see <u>Drei Lieder
für vierstimmigen Männer-
chor</u>.

0935 <u>Oh! Weep for Thee</u>
2. TTBB
3. Maurice Arnold
5. P.L. Jung, 1898

0936 <u>The Rose and the
Garden</u>, Op. 3, No. 2, 1897
2. TTBB
3. Austin Dobson
5. P.L. Jung, 1897; Schmidt
N.B.: written under pseud.
Edgar Thorn(e).

0937 <u>Schweitzerlied</u>: see
<u>Drei Lieder für vierstim-
migen Männerchor</u>.

0938 <u>Slumber Song</u>: see <u>Two
Northern Songs</u>.

0939 <u>Springtime</u>: see <u>Drei
Lieder für vierstimmigen
Männerchor</u>.

0940 <u>Sturdy and Strong</u>: see
<u>College Songs</u>.

0941 <u>Summer Wind</u>
2. SSAA
3. Richard Hovey
5. Schmidt, 1902

0942 <u>Thy Beaming Eyes</u>
2. SSAA

3. W. H. Gardner
5. Schmidt, 1919; Belwin,
1949

0943 same for TTBB
5. Schmidt

0944 <u>Two Northern Songs</u>,
Op. 43, 1890-91
2. SATB
3. MacDowell
5. Schmidt, 1891
a. The Brook
b. Slumber Song

0945 same (<u>The Brook</u> only)
2. SSA
5. Schmidt, 1891, 1917

0946 <u>Two Songs from the
Thirteenth Century</u>, 1897
2. TTBB
3. see below
5. Schmidt, 1897
a. Winter Wraps His
Grimmest Spell
(after Neidhart von
Reuental)
b. As the Gloaming
Shadows Creep (after
Frauenlot)

0947 <u>A Voice From the Sea</u>,
Op. 52, No. 2, 1897
2. TTBB
3. MacDowell
5. Schmidt
6. Columbia University

0948 <u>War Song</u>, Op. 6, 1898
2. TTBB
3. MacDowell
5. P.L. Jung, 1898; Schmidt
N.B.: written under pseud.
Edgar Thorn(e).

MACDOWELL

0949   same for SATB
5.   Schmidt, 1918

0950   We Love Thee Well,
Manhattanland: see College
Songs.

0951   Winter Wraps His Grimmest Spell: see Two Songs
from the Thirteenth   Century.

0952   The Witch, Op. 5, 1897
2.   TTBB
3.   MacDowell
5.   P.L. Jung, 1898; Schmidt
N.B.:   written under pseud.
Edgar Thorn(e).

M A S O N, L.

0953   Aulis
2.   SATB/SATB
6.   Yale

0954   Blessed Be the Lord
God, the God of Israel
2.   SATB
3.   biblical
5.   J.H. Wilkins and R. B.
Carter, 1842

0955   Christ Hath Arisen
2.   SATB
3.   E.A. Washburn
5.   Mason Bros., 1863

6.   Yale

0956   Christmas Carol
2.   SATB ?
3.   Marie Mason
6.   Yale

0957   Columbia's Birthday,
Again We Behold
2.   SATB
3.   H.F. Gould
5.   Shelpley and Wright,
1836
6.   Yale

0958   The Coronation, 1872

0959   Duty's Call, 1868
2.   SAT
3.   Sadie E. Owen

0960   Elegy of David
2.   SATB

0961   For Freedom, Honor,
and Native Land: see
Three Patriotic Songs.

0962   For Thee, My Native
Land, for Thee: see Three
Patriotic Songs.

0963   Gloria in excelsis
2.   SATB
5.   A.J. Wright, 1844

0964   God Bless Our Native
Land: see Three Patriotic
Songs.

MASON, L.

0965 Hed
2. SATB
6. L of C

0966 Hymn. God Bless Our
Native Land: see Songs
Prepared for the City Cele-
bration of Fourth of July.

0967 I Was Glad When They
Said Unto Me, 1842
2. SATB
3. biblical
5. A.B. Kidder, 1842; A.J.
Wright, 1842

0968 The Little Pilgrims
2. SATB

0969 The Lord Is in His Holy
Temple
2. SATB, organ
5. Boonin, 1977

0970 The Lord's Prayer
2. TTBB
3. biblical
5. Ditson, 1829, 1903

0971 My Native Land, 1844
2. SAB
5. A. J. Wright, 1844

0972 Ode, 1835?
2. SATB
3. Grenville Mellon and
Park Benjamin

0973 Ode. Thrice Hail,

Happy Day: see Songs
Prepared for the City
Celebration of Fourth of
July.

0974 Ode. When Stern Op-
pression's Iron Rod: see
Songs Prepared for the
City Celebration of Fourth
of July.

0975 Our Labor Here Is
Done, 1869
2. SATB
3. Lotta L. Noyes

0976 Press Forward
2. SATB

0977 Psalm 100
2. SATB
3. biblical

0978 Psalm 135
2. SATB
3. biblical

0979 Sentence
2. SATB

0980 Song of Farewell for
the Westfield, Mass. State
Normal School, 1870
2. SATB
3. Harriet E. Leonard

0981 Songs Prepared for the
City Celebration of Fourth
of July, 1845
2. SATB
5. A. B. Kidder, 1845
    a. Ode. Thrice Hail,
        Happy Day

MASON, L.

    b. Ode. When Stern Op-
        pression's Iron Rod
    c. Hymn. God Bless Our
        Native Land

0982 Thanksgiving Anthem
2. SATB
3. biblical
5. A.B. Kidder, 1840; A.J.
    Wright, 1840; Jenks and
    Palmer, 1840

0983 Three Patriotic Songs
2. SATB
5. Tappan and Dennet, 1842
    a. For Thee, My Native
        Land, for Thee
    b. For Freedom, Honor,
        and Native Land
    c. God Bless Our Native
        Land

0984 Two Sanctuses and
Anthems
2. SATB
3. biblical/liturgical
5. Ward and Co., n.d.

0985 Watchman Tell Us of the
Night
2. 3 soli, SATB, piano
3. Bowring
5. C. Bradlee, 1830

0986 Wedding Hymn
2. solo, SATB
3. Ray Palmer
5. A.J. Wright, n.d.

MASON, W.

0987 Cheerfulness
2. SATB
5. The Social Glee Book,
    Mason and Law, 1847

0988 The Complaint
2. SATB
5. The Social Glee Book,
    Mason and Law, 1847

0989 Fireside Harmony, 1848
2. SATB
3. various
5. Tappan, Whittemore, and
    Mason, 1848

0990 Give Thanks to God, He
Reigns on High
2. SATB
3. biblical
6. L of C

0991 Gondolier's Serenade
2. SATB
5. The Glee Hive, Mason and
    Law, 1851

0992 Oh Come to Me
2. SATB
5. The Social Glee Book,
    Mason and Law, 1847

0993 Serenade
2. SATB
5. The Social Glee Book,
    Mason and Law, 1847

0994 When Spring Is
Calling, 1851
2. SATB

MASON, W.

3. English
5. The Glee Hive, Mason and
    Law, 1851

P A I N E

0995 The Birds of
      Aristophanes, 1901
2. T solo, TTBB, orchestra
3. Aristophanes, trans.
    Austin Hale Evans
4. 25 minutes
5. G. Schirmer, 1901, 1902
6. Harvard

0996 Centennial Hymn, Op.
      27, 1876
2. SATB/TTBB, orchestra
3. John Greenleaf Whittier
5. Ditson, 1876
6. Harvard (score); Boston
    Public Lib. (vocal score)

0997 Columbus March and
      Hymn, 1892
2. SATB, piano
3. Paine
4. 15 minutes
5. Ditson, 1892
6. Harvard
7. 058, 087

0998 Domine salvum fac
      praesidem nostrum, Op. 8,
      1863
2. TTBB, orchestra
5. Harvard Univ. Press,
    1915

6. Harvard

0999 Freedom Our Queen
2. SATB, orchestra
3. Oliver Wendell Holmes
5. Novello, 1893, 1902
6. Harvard Musical Assoc.

1000 Funeral Hymn for a
      Soldier, Op. 14, No. 1,
      1862
2. TTBB
5. unpublished
6. Harvard

1001 Hymn, 1876
2. SATB
3. John Greenleaf Whittier
6. L of C (vocal parts)

1002 Hymn for Harvard Com-
      mencement, 1862, rev. 1883
2. unison voices
3. James Bradstreet
    Greenbough
5. Cambridge, 1885
6. Harvard

1003 Hymn of the West, 1903
2. SATB, orchestra
3. Edmund Clarence Stedman
5. Thiebes-Stierlin, 1904
6. Harvard

1004 Mass in D, Op. 10,
      1866-67
2. SATB soli, SATB,
    orchestra, organ
3. liturgical
4. 100-120 minutes
5. G. Schirmer, 1866, 1872
6. Harvard (holograph); L
    of C (mss. copy)
7. 013, 039, 058, 060, 069,
    105, 127

PAINE

1005 Minstrel's Song, Op.
14, No. 3, 1863
2. TTBB
3. Chatterton
6. L of C

1006 The Nativity, Op. 38,
1883; rev. 1903 as Op. 39
2. SATB soli, SATB,
orchestra
3. John Milton
4. 40 minutes
5. Schmidt, 1883, 1903
6. Harvard
7. 122

1007 O Bless the Lord My
Soul
2. TTBB
3. Isaac Watts
5. Boston Music Co., 1911

1008 Oedipus Tyrannus of
Sophocles, Op. 35, 1881
2. TTBB, orchestra
3. Sophocles
4. 50 minutes
5. Schmidt, 1881, 1895,
1903, 1908
6. Harvard; New England
Cons.
7. 058, 105, 122

1009 Peace, Peace to Him
that's Gone, 1863?
2. TTBB
6. Harvard

1010 Phoebus Arise, Op. 37,
1882
2. T solo, TTBB, orchestra
3. William Henry Drummond
4. 11 minutes
5. Schmidt, 1882
6. Harvard (full score and

parts); L of C (piano
vocal score)
7. 122

1011 Radway's Ready Relief,
1863
2. B solo, TTBB
5. Ditson, 1883
6. Harvard (autograph copy
of first edition)
N.B.: composed under the
pseud. of Dr. Dolore.

1012 The Realm of Fancy,
Op. 36, 1882?
2. SATB soli, SATB,
orchestra
3. John Keats
4. 10 minutes
5. Schmidt, 1882
6. Harvard (full score);
Boston Public Lib.
(piano-vocal score)
7. 122

1013 St. Peter, Op. 20,
1872
2. SATB soli, SATB,
orchestra
3. biblical
4. 90 minutes
5. Ditson, 1872
6. Harvard
7. 009, 013, 039, 058, 069,
085, 093, 123, 127

1014 Scenes from the Birds
of Aristophanes: see The
Birds of Aristophanes.

1015 Sodales cotteriani cum
carminibus nataliciis
farlovio suo S.P.D., 16
Jan 1882
4. 12-15 minutes
5. Cambridge ?, 1882
6. Harvard

BIBLIOGRAPHY OF WRITINGS

PAINE

1016 Soldier's Oath, 1865
2. TTBB
3. C. T. Brooks
5. Harvard College, 1865

1017 Song of Promise, Op.
  43, 1888
2. S solo, SATB, orchestra,
  organ
3. George Edward Woodbury
4. 45 minutes
5. Church, 1888
6. Harvard (holograph); L of
  C (mss. copy)
7. 021

1018 Summons to Love, 1882
2. TTBB
3. William Henry Drummond
6. L of C

1019 The Summer Webs
2. TTBB
6. Harvard

P A R K E R, H.

1020 A.D. 1919, Op. 84, 1919
2. S solo, SATB, orchestra
3. Brian Hooker
4. 20 minutes
5. Yale Univ. Press, 1919
6. Yale

1021 Adstant angelorum
  chori, Op. 45, 1899?
2. SATB/SATB

3. Thomas à Kempis; trans.
  Isabella Parker
7. 069

1022 Alice Brand, Op. 76,
  1913
2. SATB soli, SSA, piano
3. Sir Walter Scott
4. 20 minutes
5. G. Schirmer, 1913;
  Boston Music Co., 1913
6. Yale

1023 An Allegory of War and
  Peace, 1916
2. SATB, band
3. Francis Hartman Markoe
4. 15 minutes
6. Yale

1024 An Even Song, 1901
2. SA, piano
3. Celia Thaxter

1025 At the Mid Hours of
  Night: see Three Irish
  Folk Songs.

1026 Awake, My Lady Sweet-
  lips: see Three Part-
  songs.

1027 The Ballad of a Knight
  and His Daughter: see
  Ballade.

1028 Ballade, Op. 6, 1884
2. SATB, orchestra
3. Friederich Leopold Graf
  zu Stolberg; trans.
  Isabella Parker
4. 15 minutes
5. G. Schirmer, 1891
6. Yale

PARKER, H.

1029 Before the Heavens Were
  Spread Abroad: see Six
  Anthems.

1030 Behold How Good and
  Joyful: see Four Choruses.

1031 Behold, Ye Despisers,
  1899
2. B solo, SATB, organ
3. biblical
5. Novello, 1899

1032 Blest Are the Departed:
  see Four Choruses.

1033 Blow, Blow Thou Winter
  Wind, Op. 14, 1888
2. TTBB, piano
3. Shakespeare
5. G. Schirmer, 1892, 1908
6. Yale

1034 Bow Down Thine Ear,
  1890
2. SATB, organ
3. biblical
5. G. Schirmer, 1890

1035 Brightest and Best
2. S solo, SATB, organ
3. Reginald Heber
5. G. Schirmer, 1904

1036 Calm on the Listening
  Ear of Night, 1898
2. ST soli, SATB, organ
3. Edmund Hamilton Sears
5. The Churchman (10 Dec
  1898); Novello, 1900

6. Yale

1037 Cantus peregrinus:
  see A Wanderer's Psalm.

1038 Christ Our Passover,
  1890
2. SATB, organ
5. American Music Co.,
  1890; H. W. Gray, 1908
6. Yale

1039 Collegiate Overture,
  Op. 72, 1911
2. TTBB, orchestra
4. private printing, 1911
6. Yale

1040 Come Away!, Op. 54b,
  1901
2. SATB
3. John Dowland
5. Novello, 1901

1041 Come, Come Is the
  Swallow: see Seven Pas-
  toral Greek Scenes.

1042 Come, Gentles, Rise,
  1905
2. unison voices, piano
3. David J. Evans
5. The Churchman, 1903; G.
  Schirmer, 1905; Boston
  Music Co., 1914

1043 Come See the Place,
  1893
2. SBar soli, SATB, organ
5. G. Schirmer, 1893

PARKER, H.

1044 The Despairing Lover
2. TTBB
3. William Walsh
5. Galaxy, 1941

1045 Deus misereatur in E,
1890
2. SATB, organ
3. biblical
5. G. Schirmer, 1890, 1891

**1046 The Dream-King and His
Love**, Op. 31, 1891
2. T solo, SATB, orchestra
3. Emmanuel Geibel; trans.
Emily Whitney
4. 15 minutes
5. G. Schirmer, 1893
6. Yale

1047 The Dream of Mary, Op.
82, 1918
2. SAB soli, SATB, children's chorus, congregation, orchestra, organ
3. John Jay Chapman
4. 45 minutes
5. H.W. Gray, 1918

1048 Ecclesia, 1889
2. SATB soli, SATB, SSA,
piano
4. 20 minutes
6. Yale

1049 Far from the World,
1896
2. ST soli, SATB, organ
3. Cowper
5. Charles S. Elliott, 1896;
Novello, 1901

**1050 The Fisher: see Two
Partsongs.**

1051 Five Partsongs, Op. 2,
1882
5. unpublished

1052 Four Choruses, Op. 39,
1893
2. TTBB
5. G. Schirmer, 1894
6. Yale
a. Behold How Good and
Joyful
b. Lord Dismiss Us With
Thy Blessing
c. Softly Now the Light
of Day
d. Blest are the Departed

1053 Four Partsongs, Op.
39: see **Four Choruses.**

1054 Freedom Our Queen:
see **School Songs.**

1055 Give Unto the Lord,
1891
2. S solo, SATB, organ
5. Novello, 1891

1056 Gloriosa patria, 1915
2. SATB
3. Helene H. Boll
5. G. Schirmer, 1915

**1057 God that Makest Earth
and Heaven**
2. SATB, organ
6. L of C

PARKER, H.

1058   The Golden Stars Are
Quiring in the West: see
Seven Pastoral Greek
Scenes.

1059   Grant, We Beseech Thee,
1898
2.   SATB
3.   liturgical
5.   Boston Music Co.,   G.
Schirmer, 1898

1060   Greek Festival Hymn:
see Hymnos Andron.

1061   Harold Harfager, Op.
26, 1891
2.   A solo, SATB, orchestra
3.   anonymous
5.   G. Schirmer, 1891
6.   Yale

1062   He Faileth Not, 1919
2.   ST soli, SATB, organ
3.   Frances Ridley Havergal
5.   H. W. Gray, 1919

1063   He Who Hath Led Will
Lead
2.   S solo, SATB, organ
6.   Yale

1064   The Holy Child, Op. 37,
1893
2.   STB soli, SATB, piano or
organ
3.   Isabella Parker (from
Bible)
4.   20 minutes
5.   G. Schirmer, 1893
6.   Yale
7.   069

1065   Hora novissima, Op.
30, 1893
2.   SATB soli, SATB,
orchestra
3.   Bernard de Morlaix; arr.
Isabella Parker
4.   60 minutes
5.   Novello, 1893, 1900; Da
Capo, 1972
6.   Yale (holograph); L of C
(autograph copy)
7.   002, 028, 069, 106, 121,
127

1066   Hymn for the Victorius
Dead
2.   SATB?
3.   Hermann Hagedorn
5.   The Outlook, 1918

1067   Hymnos Andron, Op. 53,
1901
2.   TBar soli, TTBB,
orchestra
3.   Thomas Dwight Goodell
4.   30 minutes
5.   G. Schirmer, 1901
6.   Yale
7.   028

1068   I Remember, 1923
2.   SSA, piano
3.   Henry W. Longfellow
5.   A Book of Choruses,
Silver Burdett, 1923

1069   I Remember the Black
Wharfs and Ships: see
Songs for Parker Daugh-
ters.

1070   I Shall Not Die but
Live, 1905
2.   Bar solo, SATB, organ
3.   biblical
5.   Ditson, 1905

PARKER, H.

1071 I Will Set His Dominion
in the Sea, 1891
2. SATB, organ
5. Novello, 1891

1072 I Will Twine the Violet: see Seven Pastoral
Greek Scenes.

1073 Idylle, Op. 15, 1886
2. TBar soli, SATB,
orchestra
3. Goethe; trans. Isabella
Parker
4. 10 minutes
5. G. Schirmer, 1891
6. Yale

1074 In Yonder Cool, Green
Dell
2. TTBB
3. trans. Theodore Baker
5. G. Schirmer, 1895

1075 In Heavenly Love
Abiding: see Six Anthems.

1076 In Loud Exalted Strains
2. SATB
5. Novello, 1892
6. L of C

1077 In May, 1897; rev. 1904
2. SSAA, harp, orchestra
3. textless
5. G. Schirmer, 1897
6. Yale

1078 It Was a Lover and His
Lass, 1915
2. SS, violin, piano

3. Shakespeare
6. Yale

1079 Jubilate Deo: see Six
Anthems.

1080 Jubilee Hymn, 1899
2. SATB, organ
3. David J. Evans
6. L of C

1081 King Gorm the Grim,
Op. 64, 1906-1908
2. SATB, orchestra
3. Theodore Fontane; trans.
Marian Parker Whitney
4. 18 minutes
5. G. Schirmer, 1908, 1910
6. Yale (holograph); L of C
(autograph)

1082 King Trojan: see
König Trojan.

1083 Kitty Magel: see
Three Irish Folk Songs.

1084 The Kobolds, Op. 21,
1890
2. SATB, orchestra
3. Arlo Bates
4. 10 minutes
5. Novello, 1891
6. Yale

1085 König Trojan, Op. 8,
1885
2. SATB soli, SATB,
orchestra
3. Fr. A. Muth
4. 30 minutes
5. Schmidt, 1886
6. Yale
7. 028, 122

PARKER, H.

1086   The Lamp in the West:
see Three Partsongs.

1087   Laus artium, 1898
2. solo, SATB, orchestra
3. Eva J. O'Meara
4. 40 minutes
6. Yale

1088   The Leap of a Roushan
Beg, Op. 75, 1913
2. T solo, TTBB, orchestra
3. Henry W. Longfellow
4. 12 minutes
5. G. Schirmer, 1913;
Boston Music Co., 1913

1089   The Legend of St.
Christopher, Op. 43, 1897
2. STB soli, SATB,
orchestra, organ
3. Isabella Parker
4. 90 minutes
5. Novello, 1898; H. W.
Gray,1898
6. Yale
7. 028, 069

1090   Let Us Rise Up and
Build, 1892
2. SBar soli, SATB, organ,
brass, harp, timp.
3. biblical
6. Yale; New York Public
Lib. (xerox copy)

1091   Light's Glittering
Morn, 1894
2. B solo, SATB, organ
3. St. Ambrose; trans. J.
M. Neale
4. 10 minutes

5. G. Schirmer, 1894
6. Yale

1092   Lord Dismiss Us with
Thy Blessing: see Four
Choruses.

1093   The Lord Is My Light,
1890
2. SATB, organ
3. biblical
5. G. Schirmer, 1890

1094   The Lord is My Shepherd: see Psalm 23.

1095   Love! I Cry, the Truant Love!: see Seven Pastoral Greek Scenes.

1096   Magnificat in E-flat,
1890
2. solo, SATB, organ
3. biblical
5. G. Schirmer, 1890

1097   Magnificat and Nunc
dimittis in E-flat, Op.
34b, 1893
2. SATB, organ
3. liturgical/biblical
5. Novello, 1893

1098   The Morning and Evening Service in E, with the
Office For the Holy Com-
munion, Op. 18, 1890
2. SATB, organ
3. liturgical
4. 45-50 minutes
5. Novello, 1892
6. Yale

PARKER, H.

1099 Morven and the Grail,
Op. 79, 1915
2. SATB soli, SATB,
orchestra
3. Brian Hooker
4. 110 minutes
5. Boston Music Co., 1915

1100 Mountain Shepherd's
Song, Op. 1, 1883
2. TTBB, piano
3. Uhland; trans. James A.
Beatley
5. Russell Bros., 1884
6. Yale

1101 My Love: see Three
Choruses.

1102 National Hymn
2. SATB
3. D. C. Roberts
5. A Book of Choruses,
Silver Burdett, 1923

1103 The Night Has a Thousand Eyes: see Three Partsongs.

1104 The Norsemen's Raid:
see Normanenzug.

1105 Normanenzug, Op. 16,
1888
2. TTBB, orchestra
3. Herman von Lingg; trans.
Emily Whitney
4. 15 minutes
5. Church, 1911
6. Yale

1106 Now Sinks the Sun:
see Six Anthems.

1107 Nunc dimittis in E-
flat, 1890
2. SATB, organ
3. liturgical
5. G. Schirmer, 1890

1108 Nunc dimittis in E-
flat, 1893:   see Magnificat and Nunc dimittis in
E-flat.

1109 O Lord, I Will Exalt
Thee, 1897
2. SATB soli, SATB, organ
3. biblical
5. G. Schirmer, 1897
6. Yale

1110 O 'Twas a Joyful Sound
2. SATB
3. S. B. Whitney?
5. Ditson, n.d.

1111 Ode for Commencement
Day at Yale University,
Op. 42, 1895
2. TTBB, piano
3. Edmund Clarence Stedman
4. 10 minutes
5. G. Schirmer, 1895
6. Yale

1112 Ode for the Dedication
of the Albright Art Gal-
lery, Buffalo, NY
2. TTBB, orchestra or band
3. anonymous
5. G. Schirmer, 1905

PARKER, H.

1113 Office for the Holy
Communion in E: see The
Morning and Evening Ser-
vice.

1114 The Office for the Holy
Communion in B-flat, Op.
57, 1904
2. S solo, SATB, organ
3. liturgical
4. 12-15 minutes
5. Novello, 1904

1115 Piscatrix, 1907
2. TTBB
3. D. H. Holmes
5. G. Schirmer, 1908
6. Yale

1116 Processional Hymn, 1893

1117 Psalm 23: The Lord is
My Shepherd, Op. 3, 1884?
2. S solo, SSAA, organ, harp
3. biblical
4. 10 minutes
5. G. Schirmer, 1904
6. Yale
7. 028

1118 The Red Cross Spirit
Speaks
2. SATB
3. John Finley
5. H.W. Gray, 1918

1119 same for SSAA

1120 same for TTBB

1121 Rejoice in the Lord,
1898
2. SATB, organ
3. Charles Wesley and John
Taylor and Thomas Kelley
5. Ditson, 1894; C. W.
Thompson, 1898

1122 The Riven Tomb, 1891
2. SATB, organ
5. New York Herald (29
March 1891, p. 11)

1123 The Robbers, 1901
2. SATB, piano
3. Joanna Baillie
4. 20 minutes
5. The Laurel Song Book, C.
C. Birchard Co., 1901

1124 Rollicking Robin: see
Songs for Parker Daugh-
ters.

1125 St. Christopher: see
The Legend of St. Chris-
topher.

1126 School Songs, Op. 66
2. SATB, piano
3. see below
5. "d" in A Book of Choruses, Silver Burdett,
1923
a. (not published)
b. Springtime Revelries
(Nixon Waterman)
c. The Storm (Waterman)
d. Freedom, Our Queen
(Oliver Wendell
Holmes)

1127 September Gale: see
Songs for Parker Daugh-
ters.

PARKER, H.

1128 Seven Pastoral Greek
 Scenes, Op. 74, 1908-1912
2. SA soli, SSAA, oboe,
 harp, strings or piano
3. after Meleager and
 Argentarius
4. 20 minutes
5. G. Schirmer, 1913
6. Yale
 a. The Windy Winter From
 the Sky Is Gone
 b. I Will Twine the
 Violet
 c. Come, Come Is the
 Swallow
 d. White Flowers the
 Violet Now
 e. Sweet On the Pipe, By
 Pan of Arcady
 f. Love! I Cry the
 Truant Love!
 g. The Golden Stars Are
 Quiring in the West

1129 The Shan Van: see
 Three Irish Folk Songs.

1130 The Shepherd's Vision,
 Op. 63, 1906
2. S or T, B soli, SATB,
 organ, oboe, strings,
 harp
3. Frank van der Stucken;
 trans. Alice C. Jennings
4. 15 minutes
5. H.W. Gray, 1906
7. 069

1131 Six Anthems, 1893-1909
2. SATB soli, SATB, organ
3. see below
5. Novello, 1893; H.W.
 Gray, 1900-37
 a. To Whom Then Will Ye
 Liken God

 b. Now Sinks the Sun
 c. In Heavenly Love
 Abiding (Anna L.
 Waring)
 d. Before the Heavens
 Were Spread Abroad
 e. Jubilate Deo
 f. They that Go Down in
 Ships

1132 Six Partsongs, Op. 33:
 see Three Choruses (re-
 maining three numbers not
 published).

1133 Softly Now the Light
 of Day: see Four Chor-
 uses.

1134 Songs for Parker
 Daughters, 1911
2. SSAA
3. see below
6. Yale
 a. I Remember the Black
 Wharfs and Ships
 (Henry W. Long-
 fellow)
 b. September Gale (C.
 H. Crandall)
 c. Rollicking Robin (L.
 Larcom)
 d. (not published)

1135 Song of a Pilgrim
 Soul, 1912
2. SSA, piano
3. Henry Van Dyke
5. Scribners, 1911

1136 A Song of Times, Op.
 73, 1911
2. S solo, SATB, bugle
 corps, band/orchestra,
 organ
3. John Luther Long

PARKER, H.

4. 12 minutes
5. G. Schirmer, 1911

1137 Spirit of Beauty, Op.
61, 1905
2. TTBB, band/orchestra
3. Arthur Detmers
4. 10-12 minutes
5. G. Schirmer, 1905
6. Yale
7. 021

1138 Springtime Revelrie:
see School Songs.

1139 A Star Song, Op. 54,
1902
2. SATB soli, SATB,
orchestra
3. Henry Bernard Carpenter
4. 25 minutes
5. Church, 1902

1140 The Storm: see School
Songs.

1141 Sweet on the Pipe, by
Pan of Arcady: see Seven
Pastoral Greek Scenes.

1142 Te Deum in E
2. SATB, organ
3. liturgical
5. Novello, 19?

1143 Te Deum in A, 1891
2. SATB, organ
3. liturgical
5. G. Schirmer, 1891

1144 Te Deum laudamus in B-
flat, 1893
2. SATB, organ
3. liturgical
5. G. Schirmer, 1893

1145 There Is a Land of
Pure Delight, 1890
2. solo, SATB, organ

1146 They That Go Down To
the Sea In Ships: see Six
Anthems.

1147 Thou Shalt Remember,
1901
2. Bar solo, SATB, organ
5. Novello, 1901

1148 Three Choruses, Op.
33, 1893
2. TTBB
3. see below
5. G. Schirmer, 1893
   a. My Love (L.E.
      Mitchell)
   b. Three Words (William
      Barclay Dunham)
   c. Valentine (C.G.
      Blanden)

1149 Three Irish Folk Songs
2. TTBB
3. see below
5. G. Schirmer, 1908
   a. The Shan Van Voght
      (anonymous)
   b. At the Mid Hours of
      Night (Thomas Moore)
   c. Kitty Magel (Frances
      A. Fahy)

1150 Three Partsongs, Op.
48, 1901

PARKER, H.

2. TTBB
3. see below
5. Church, 1901
   a. Awake, My Lady
      Sweetlips (Ella
      Higginson)
   b. The Lamp in the West
      (E. Higginson)
   c. The Night Has a
      Thousand Eyes
      (Francis W.
      Bourdillon)

1151 Three Words: see **Three Choruses.**

1152 To Whom Then Will Ye Liken God: see **Six Anthems.**

1153 Traumkönig und sein Lieb: see **Dream-king and His Love.**

1154 Triumphal March, 1919
2. SATB, piano
3. D.K. Stevens
5. High School Song Book, G. Parsons

1155 Two Partsongs, Op. 27, 1892?
2. SSAA, piano
3. see below
5. Boston Music Co., 1892
   a. The Fisher (Goethe)
   b. The Water Fay
      (Heinrich Heine)

1156 Union and Liberty, Op. 60, 1905

2. SATB, band/orchestra
3. Oliver Wendell Holmes
4. 10 minutes
5. G. Schirmer, 1905
6. Yale

1157 Valentine: see **Three Choruses.**

1158 The Voice That Breathed O'er Eden, 1916
2. SATB
6. Yale

1159 A Wanderer's Psalm (Cantus peregrinus), Op. 50, 1900
2. SATB soli, SATB, orchestra
3. anonymous
4. 50 minutes
5. Novello, 1900
6. Yale

1160 The Water Fay: see **Two Partsongs.**

1161 While We Have Time, 1900
2. S solo, SSAA, organ
5. Novello, 1900

1162 White Flowers the Violet Now: see **Seven Pastoral Greek Scenes.**

1163 Who Shall Roll Us Away the Stone?, 1891
2. S solo, SATB, organ
3. biblical
4. 12 minutes
5. M. Leidt and Co., 1891

PARKER, H.

1164 The Windy Winter from
the Sky ls Gone: see Seven
Pastoral Greek Scenes.

P A R K E R, J.C.D.

1165 Benedic, anima mea in E
2. SATB, organ
3. liturgical
5. The Parish Choir,
Medford, Mass., 1878

1166 Benedictus in C
2. SATB, organ
3. liturgical
5. The Parish Choir, 1876;
Ditson, 1880

1167 Benedictus in E
2. S solo, SATB, organ
3. biblical
5. Ditson, 1880

1168 Benedictus in F
2. A solo, SATB, organ
3. liturgical
5. Ditson, 1880

1169 Benedictus in B-flat
2. SATB, organ
3. liturgical
5. Ditson, 1880

1170 Benedictus and Kyrie in
E-flat
2. B solo, SATB, organ

1171 The Blind King, 1883
2. Bar solo, TTBB,
orchestra
3. after Uhland
4. 12 minutes
5. Ditson, 1883

1172 Bugle Song: see Seven
Part Songs.

1173 Cantate Domino in G
2. SATB, organ
3. biblical
5. The Parish Choir, 1881

1174 Christmas Anthem in F
2. T solo, SATB, organ
3. biblical
4. 10 minutes
5. Ditson, 1879

1175 Daybreak: see Seven
Partsongs.

1176 Deus misereatur in A
2. SATB, organ
3. biblical
5. The Parish Choir, 1879;
Ditson, 1880
6. New England Cons.

1177 Easter Anthem in E-
flat
2. SATB soli, SATB, organ
3. biblical
5. Ditson, 1880

1178 Easter Anthem in G
2. SATB, organ
3. biblical
5. Ditson, 1880

PARKER, J.C.D.

1179 Easter Anthem in A
2. SATB, organ
3. biblical
5. Ditson, 1880

1180 Gay and Sad: see Seven
Partsongs.

1181 Jubilate in D
2. SATB, organ
3. biblical
5. Ditson, 1880

1182 Jubilate in E, No. 1
2. SATB, organ
3. biblical
5. Ditson, 1880

1183 Jubilate in E, No. 2
2. SATB, organ
3. biblical
5. Ditson, 1880

1184 Jubilate in G
2. SATB soli, SATB, organ
3. biblical
5. Ditson, 1880

1185 The Life of Man, 1894
2. SATB soli, SATB,
   orchestra
4. 90 minutes
5. Schmidt, 1894
6. New England Cons. (full
   score); L of C (auto-
   graph vocal score)

1186 The Lord Is My Shepherd
6. New England Cons.

1187 Psalm 137
2. S solo, SATB, orchestra
3. biblical
4. 10 minutes
6. L of C
7. 069

1188 Redemption Hymn, 1877
2. A solo, SATB, orchestra
3. anonymous
4. 15 minutes
5. Ditson, 1877, 1914
7. 069, 122

1189 The River Sprite: see
Seven Partsongs.

1190 St. John, 1890
2. SATB soli, SATB,
   orchestra
3. biblical; arr. Parker
4. 20 minutes
5. Schmidt, 1890
6. New England Cons.
7. 069

1191 Sanctus
6. New England Cons.

1192 The Sea Hath its
Pearls: see Seven Part-
songs.

1193 Seven Partsongs, 1875
2. SATB, piano
3. see below
5. Ditson, 1875
   a. The Sea Hath its
       Pearls (Heine, arr.
       Longfellow)
   b. The World's Wan-
       derer's (Percy
       Bysshe Shelley)
   c. Bugle Song (Alfred
       Lord Tennyson)
   d. The River Sprite
       (William Cullan

PARKER, J.C.D.

5. Ditson, 1880

     Bryant)
e. Gay and Sad (Charles
    J. Sprague)
f. Daybreak (Henry W.
    Longfellow)

1201 Te Deum in A
2. SATB, organ
3. liturgical;
4. 10 minutes
5. Ditson, 1880

1194 Te Deum in C
2. SATB, organ
3. liturgical
5. Ditson, 1880

1202 Te Deum in B-flat
2. SATB, organ
3. liturgical
4. 10 minutes
5. Ditson, 1880

1195 Te Deum in D
2. SATB, organ
3. liturgical
5. Ditson, 1880

1203 The West Wind: see
Seven Partsongs.

1196 Te Deum in E-flat
2. SATB, organ
3. liturgical
5. Ditson, 1880

1204 The World's Wander-
er's: see Seven Part-
songs.

1197 Te Deum in E, No. 1
2. SATB, organ
3. liturgical
5. Ditson, 1880

R O O T

1198 Te Deum in E, No. 2
2. T solo, SATB, organ
3. liturgical
4. 10 minutes
5. Ditson, 1880

1205 Belshazzar's Feast,
1860
2. SATB soli, SATB,
narrator, orchestra
3. Gen. B.F. Edwards
4. 30 minutes
5. Ditson, 1888; Mason
Bros., 1860
7. 069

1199 Te Deum in F
2. A solo, SATB, organ
3. liturgical
5. Ditson, 1880

1200 Te Deum in G
2. ST soli, SATB, organ
3. liturgical

1206 Bethlehem
2. SATB soli, SATB,
orchestra
3. Frederick E. Weatherly
4. 35 minutes
5. Church, 1889

ROOT

1207   The Captivity and Restoration: see Daniel.

1208   The Choicest Gift
2. SATB soli, SATB, 10 readers, keyboard
5. Church, 1883
7. 069

1209   Columbus, the Hero of Faith, 1892
2. SATB soli, SATB, keyboard
3. Hezekiah Butterworth
4. 50 minutes
5. Church, 1893?
7. 021

1210   Daniel; or, The Captivity and Restoration
2. SATB soli, SATB, piano
3. C.M. Cady and Frances Jane Crosby
4. 30 minutes
5. Church, 1882; Mason, 185?; Ditson, 1881
7. 069
N.B.: composed jointly with Wm. B. Bradbury

1211   David, the Shepherd Boy
2. SATB soli, SATB, children's choir (optional), piano
3. Hezekiah Butterworth
4. 25 minutes
5. Church, 1882

1212   Faith Triumphant; or, The Healings of Naaman, 1886
2. SSATB soli, SATB, orchestra
3. Hezekiah Butterworth
4. 50 minutes
5. Church, 1886

7. 069

1213   The Fall of Babylon: see Belshazzar's Feast.

1214   Florens; or, The Pilgrims; or, The Children of the Plain
2. SATB
3. David Gow
4. 25 minutes
5. Church, 1890
7. 069

1215   The Flower Queen; or, The Coronation of the Rose, 1852, rev. 1880
2. SAB soli, SSA, orchestra
3. Frances Jane Crosby
4. 40 minutes
5. Mason and Law, 1852; Ditson, 1880, 1908
N.B.: revised under the new title "The New Flower Queen."

1216   Have Ye Sharpened Your Swords?
2. TTBB, piano
3. D. W. Manchester
5. Root and Cady, 1862

1217   The Haymakers, 1857
2. SSATBarB soli, SATB, keyboard
3. Root
4. 60 minutes
5. Mason Bros, 1857; Ditson, 1857; Curwen, 18?; A-R Editions, 1984
6. unknown
7. 021, 055, 064, 098

1218   The Healings of Naaman: see Faith Triumphant.

ROOT

1219   Jacob and Esau
2.   SATB soli, SATB,
     narrator, orchestra
3.   A.J. Foxwell
4.   30 minutes
5.   Church, 1890
7.   069

**1220   Phyllis, the Farmer's
Daughter, 1892**
2.   SATB soli, SATB,
     orchestra
3.   Clara Louise Burnham
4.   20 minutes
5.   Church, 1892

**1221   The Pilgrim Fathers,
1854**
2.   SATB soli, SATB, piano
3.   Frances Jane Crosby
4.   30 minutes
5.   Mason Bros., 1854

**1222   The Pillar of Fire; or,
The Return of Israel**
2.   SATB, piano
3.   Hezekiah Butterworth
4.   45 minutes
5.   Church, 1887

1223   The Song Tournament
2.   SATB soli, SATB, piano
3.   Root and Palmer
     Hartsough
4.   45 minutes
5.   Church, 1878

1224   The Star of Light
2.   SATB soli, SATB,
     keyboard
3.   James Stuart Bogg
4.   20 minutes
5.   Church, 1896

7.   069
N.B.:   composed jointly with
F. W. Root.

1225   Under the Palms
2.   SATB soli, SATB,
     children's choir,
     narrator, orchestra
7.   069

W H I T I N G, A.

**1226   Christ Our Passover,
1895?**
2.   SATB, organ
3.   biblical
5.   G. Schirmer

**1227   The Desert shall
Rejoice, 1895?**
2.   SATB, organ
3.   biblical
5.   G. Schirmer

**1228   Five Settings of the
Venite, exultemus Domino,
1897**
2.   SATB, organ
3.   liturgical
4.   15 minutes (total)
5.   G. Schirmer

**1229   Give Ear, O Shepherd
of Israel**
2.   SATB, organ
3.   biblical
5.   Novello

**1230   Gracious Is the Lord,
1893**
2.   SATB, organ

WHITING, A.

3. biblical
5. G. Schirmer

1231 **Hark! What Mean Those Holy Voices?**
2. A solo, SATB, organ
3. J. Carwood
5. G. Schirmer, 1894

1232 **His Salvation Is Nigh**
2. ST soli, SATB, organ
3. biblical
5. Novello, 1903

1233 **The Hundred Pipers:** see Two Folk Songs.

1234 **I Shall Not Die but Live,** 1896?
2. SATB, organ
3. biblical
5. G. Schirmer

1235 **Into Thy Hands I Commend My Spirit:** see O God, My Heart is Ready.

1236 **Lament for Owen Roe O'Neill:** see Two Folk Songs.

1237 **Lord, Thou Hast Searched Me,** 1893?
2. T solo, SATB, organ
3. biblical
5. Novello

1238 **Mass in C Minor**

1239 **The Morning and Evening Service, Together With the Office for the Holy Communion in A,** 1896
2. SATB, organ
3. biblical/liturgical
4. 40 minutes
5. G. Schirmer

1240 **My Heart is Fixed, O God,** 1893?
2. A or B solo, SATB, organ
3. Psalm 108
5. G. Schirmer

1241 **Oh God, My Heart is Ready,** Op. 17
2. SATB
3. biblical
4. 15 minutes
5. G. Schirmer, 1899

1242 **A Serenade**
2. TTBB
6. New York Public Lib.

1243 **They that Wait Upon the Lord,** 1903?
2. Bar solo, SSATBB, organ
3. biblical
5. G. Schirmer

1244 **Thou Art Fairer than the Children of Men,** 1897?
2. SBar soli, SATB, organ
3. biblical
4. 10 minutes
5. G. Schirmer

1245 **Two Folk Songs,** 1923
2. Bar solo, TTBB, piano four-hands
3. see below
5. G. Schirmer, 1923

WHITING, A.

a. Lament for Owen Row
    O'Neill (trad. Irish)
b. The Hundred Pipers
    (Lady Nairne)

W H I T I N G, G.E.

1246 The Brooklet, 1875
2. SATB, piano ad lib.
6. Boston Public Lib.

1247 Beatus vir: see The
Vesperal Psalms.

1248 Catholic Vespers
3. liturgical
4. 15 minutes
5. Ditson, 1909

1249 Christ Our Passover
2. SATB, organ
5. Boston Cons. Music
    Store, 1885

**1250 Close Sheltered in Some
Fragrant Nook**, 187?
2. SATB
6. Boston Public Lib.

1251 Confiteor: see The
Vesperal Psalms.

1252 Dixit Dominus: see The
Vesperal Psalms.

1253 Dixit Dominus: see
Vespers of the Blessed
Virgin.

1254 Domine: see The
Vesperal Psalms.

1255 Domine: see Vespers
of the Blessed Virgin.

1256 Dream Picture, Op. 19,
    1891?
2. SATB soli, SATB,
    orchestra
3. Carl Nielson
4. 25 minutes
5. Schmidt, 1891
6. Boston Public Lib.

1257 Drinking Song, 187?
2. TTBB
6. Boston Public Lib.

1258 The Evening Star, 1873
2. SATB
6. Boston Public Lib.

1259 Festival Te Deum in C,
    1872
2. 3 solo voices, SATB,
    organ, orchestra
3. liturgical
4. 18-25 minutes
6. Boston Public Lib.

1260 Free Lances
2. TTBB, brass and
    percussion
4. 10 minutes
5. Ditson, 1882

WHITING, G.E.

1261 Golden Legend, 1870
2. solo, SATB, piano
3. Henry W. Longfellow
6. Boston Public Lib.

1262 Good Morrow, 1875
2. SATB, piano ad lib.
6. Boston Public Lib.

1263 Henry of Navarre
2. T solo, TTBB, orchestra
3. T. B. Macaulay
4. 45 minutes
5. White, Smith, and Co.,
    1885

1264 Hymn for Easter, 1885?
2. SATB, organ
5. Tourjée, 1885

1265 In exitu Israel: see
The Vesperal Psalms.

1266 Lauda Jerusalem: see
Vespers of the Blessed
Virgin.

1267 Laudate pueri: see The
Vesperal Psalms.

1268 Leonora
2. SATB soli, SATB,
    orchestra
3. G. A. Bürger; trans. A
    Baskerville
4. 42 minutes
6. Boston Public Lib.

1269 Magnificat: see

Vespers of the Blessed
Virgin.

1270 March of the Monks of
Bangor
2. TTBB, piano
3. Sir Walter Scott
4. 20 minutes
5. Church, 1887

1271 Mass in C Minor, 1869
2. SATB soli, SATB,
    orchestra, organ
3. liturgical
4. 40 minutes
6. Boston Public Lib.
7. 031 (?)

1272 Mass in C Minor, No.
1, 187?
2. SATB soli, SATB,
    orchestra, organ
3. liturgical
4. 20 minutes
6. Boston Public Lib.
7. 031 (?)

1273 Mass in F Minor, 1873-
83
2. SATB, organ
3. liturgical
4. 35 minutes
6. Boston Public Lib.

1274 Midnight
2. SATB soli, SATB,
    orchestra
3. Charles L. Hildreth
4. 15 minutes
5. Schmidt, 1893

1275 Ode: Oh Art Divine,
18?
2. SATB, organ
3. Louise C. Elson
6. Boston Public Lib.

WHITING, G.E.

1276 Our Country, Op. 60
2. SATB, piano
3. Whiting
5. Presser, 1909

1277 Psalm 24
2. SATB, piano
3. biblical, arr. Ephraim
    Cutter
5. Ginn, 1876

1278 Shed No Tear!, 1873
2. SATB, piano ad lib.
6. Boston Public Lib.

1279 The Sirens, 1873
2. SATB, piano
6. Boston Public Lib.

1280 The Tale of the Viking,
     1881?
2. STB soli, SATB,
    orchestra
3. Henry W. Longfellow
4. 70 minutes
5. G. Schirmer, 1881, 1909
7. 021, 122

1281 Traumbilder: see **Dream
    Pictures**.

1282 The Vesper Hymns, 187?
2. SATB
3. liturgical
6. Boston Public Lib.

1283 The Vesperal Psalms,
     1872
2. SATB, organ
3. liturgical
4. 15-20 minutes

5. Gramer and Co., 1887
6. Boston Public Lib.
    a. Domine
    b. Dixit Dominus
    c. Confiteor
    d. Beatus vir
    e. Laudate pueri
    f. In exitu Israel

**1284 Vespers of the Blessed
    Virgin**
2. solo voices, SATB, organ
3. liturgical
4. 20 minutes
5. Gramer and Co., 1887
    a. Domine
    b. Dixit Dominus
    c. Lauda Jerusalem
    d. Magnificat

1285 The Viking's Story:
    see **Tale of the Viking**.

1286 The Winds, 1875
2. SATB, piano
6. Boston Public Lib.

W O R K

**1287 Joy in Heaven!; or,
    The Returning Wanderer's
    Welcome**
2. soli, chorus

BIBLIOGRAPHY

BIBLIOGRAPHY OF WRITINGS
ON NINETEENTH-CENTURY AMERICAN CHORAL MUSIC

001 Anonymous. "Choral and piano works by Charles Ives issued." Musical America, 69 (June, 1949), p. 28.
Reviews the Three Harvest Home Chorales.

002 Anonymous. "Performance Reviews." Choral Guide, 7 (Jan., 1955), p. 28.
Review of a performance of H. Parker's Hora Novissima at the Fifth Ave. Presbyterian Church in N.Y.C. on 7 Nov. 1954.

003 Anonymous. "Psalm XXIV for SATB a cappella." Notes, 14 (Sept. 1957), p. 18.
Regarding the composition by Ives.

004 Allwardt, Anton Paul. Sacred Music in New York City, 1800-1850. S.M.D. dissertation, Union Theological Seminary, 1950.
Chapter Four deals with the formation of church choirs including historical precedents and contemporary attitudes towards choral singing in church.

005 Alviani, Doric. The Choral Church Music of Arthur William Foote. S.M.D. dissertation, Union Theological Seminary, 1962.
Part One is a biography of Foote. Part Two deals exclusively with the church music compositions. The Appendixes include two lists of Foote's sacred and secular music. Volume II of the dissertation is a thematic catalog of the composer's anthems, choruses, etc. An excellent source for information on these works.

006 Alwes, Chester L. "Formal Structure as a Guide to Rehearsal Strategy in 'Psalm 90' by Charles Ives." The Choral Journal, 25/8 (April, 1985), p. 21.
Alwes examines different motives in the composition and how these may be separated and used as "handles" in learning the work, as well as how Ives uses these motives to construct Psalm 90.

007 Anderson, Donna K. Charles T. Griffes: An Annotated Bibliography-Dis-

cography.   Detroit: Information Coordinators, 1977.
   In several sections: a
chronology of Griffes's life
and a separate chronology of
his published works, as well
as the bibliography.   The
discography gives listings by
recording number and genre of
composition. There is also a
listing of first performances, by composition and by
chronology, with an index to
performers.

008   Anderson, Donna K. The
Works of Charles T. Griffes:
A Descriptive Catalog.   Detroit: UMI Research Press,
1983.
   The choral music is listed
on pp. 411-420. Each choral
work cited is followed by a
lengthy annotation that includes commentary as well as
factual data.

009   Apthorp, W.F. "Music."
Atlantic Monthly, 31 (April,
1873), p. 506.
   A review of Paine's St.
Peter.   Discusses the qual-
ity of the work, in part by
taking argument with an article in The Nation of 13
Feb. 1873. The author gives
a description of the work and
discusses its text and stylistic elements.

010   Apthorp, W.F. "Music."
Atlantic Monthly, 38 (July,
1876), p. 122.
   A review of Dudley Buck's
Centennial Cantata, crit-
icizing Buck's choice of text
but generally favorable to-

wards the music.   Also includes a brief paragraph on
Paine's Whittier's Hymn.

011   Balshaw, P.A.   "The
Celestial Country: an Introduction."   The Choral
Journal, 15/7 (March, 1975,
p. 16.
   A very thorough analysis
of the composition with 12
musical examples and several
tables that clearly illus-
trate the text. Also good
background information and a
justification   for performance and study of the work.

012   Berthoud, P.   The
Musical Works of Dr. Henry
Hadley, Compiled and Listed.
New York: National Association for American Composers
and Conductors and The Henry
Hadley Foundation, 1942.
   This monograph gives two
listings of the works of the
composer, alphabetically and
then by genre, with annotations   listing   performing
forces, authors of texts,
and publishers.

013   Bialosky, Marshall.
"Some   Late   Nineteenth-
Century Members of ASUC:
Paine,   MacDowell,   and
Chadwick." ASUC Proceedings,
11-12 (1976-77), p. 40.
   Discusses the first per-
formances of Paine's Mass in
D and St. Peter and gives
some interesting information
on H. Parker's choral activ-
ities.

014   Block, Adrienne Fried.
"Why Amy Beach Succeeded as a
Composer: the Early Years."
Current   Musicology,   36
(1983), p. 41.
    Includes material on the
composer's   early   concert
life.   Contains good (and
rare) material on the **Mass**,
including a facsimile of the
original   program,   and an
excellent bibliography.

015   Block, Adrienne Fried,
Neuls-Bates, Carol. Women in
American Music: a Bibliography of Music and Literature. Westport, Conn.: Greenwood Press, 1979.
    Provides a good biblio-
graphy on all aspects of
Beach's music as well as a
complete catalog of her choral compositions (entries
nos. 1286-1346).

016   Boardman, Herbert R.
Henry Hadley, Ambassador of
Harmony.   Emory University
(Georgia):   Banner   Press,
1932.
    The choral works are
described in Chapter 8 (p.
139).

017 Boda, Daniel. The Music
of Charles T. Griffes. PhD
dissertation, University of
Florida, 1962.
    Chapter One is a biograph-
ical sketch of the composer.
The next three chapters deal
with Griffes's style, harmony, tonality, and form.
The dissertation also has a
listing of the composer's
published works.

018 Boston.   Boston Public
Library.   Music   Division.
[Beach]
    Correspondence relating
to the composition and
revision of the Op. 84 Te
Deum.

019 Boston. Boston Public
Library.   Music Division.
[Foote]
    Programs and clippings
from 1 Feb. 1879 - 17 April
1937.   Compiled by the
B.P.L. music division, 1942.

020 Boston.   Boston Public
Library.   Music Division.
[Paine]
    Letters, scrapbooks, pro-
grams, etc., compiled by the
B.P.L. music division.

021   Boulton,   J.F.
Religious   Influences   on
American Secular Cantatas.
PhD dissertation, University
of Michigan, 1965.
    Chapter One is an histor-
ical introduction to the
topic. Many of the choral
works in my study are dis-
cussed in the remaining
chapters, including: Buck:
Centennial Meditation, Paul
Revere's Ride, Voyage of
Columbus; Bristow: Great
Republic; Foote: Farewell
to Hiawatha, Wreck of the
Hesperus; Hadley: Lelawala;
Paine: Song of Promise; H.
Parker: Spirit of Beauty;
Root: Columbus, the Hero of
Faith, Haymakers, Phyllis,
the Farmer's Daughter, Pilgrim Fathers;   G. E. Whiting: Tale of the Viking.

022   Burk,   James   M.   A
Charles   Ives   Bibliography.
To be published by the Col-
lege Music Society in their
series   Bibliographies   in
American Music.

023 Bruce, Nelly. "Ives and
Nineteenth-Century   American
Music."   in An Ives Celebra-
tion, ed. H. Wiley Hitchcock
and Vivien Perlis, Urbana:
University of Illinois Press,
1977.
     Deals with possible nine-
teenth-century   influences on
Ives,   particularly Stephen
Foster and A. P. Heinrich.

024   Caldwell, James L.   The
Life   and   Works   of James
Cutler Dunn Parker. PhD dissertation, Florida State University, 1968.
     Gives a good biography of
Parker and discusses his contributions to church and choral music and music education.

025 Cambridge, Mass.   Harvard University.   Eda Kuhn
Loeb Music Library. [Paine].
     Letters, scrapbooks, pro-
grams, etc., compiled by the
Harvard Music Library.

026   Campbell,   Douglas
Graves.   George W. Chadwick:
His   Life   and Works.   PhD
dissertation, University of
Rochester, 1957.
     The   choral   works   are
discussed on pp. 46-67.   The
author deals with the anthems
for church choir as well as
the larger   choral music;
there is an especially long
section on Noël.   This is
the best analytical and descriptive guide to the works.
Includes a listing of all
the works.

027   Canfield,   John Clair,
Jr.   Henry Kimball Hadley:
His Life and Works (1871-
1937).   PhD   dissertation,
Florida   State University,
1960.
     Discusses   the works in
the context of the composer's life.   The list of
works is divided into two
parts, those with opus numbers and those without.

028   Chadwick,   George W.
Horatio Parker.   New Haven:
Yale University Press, 1921.
Reprint: New   York: AMS
Press, 1972.
     A very short book, but
with information on these
works: 23rd Psalm, König
Trojan, Hora Novissima, The
Legend of St. Christopher,
and Hymnos Andron. Does not
cover any of these in depth.

029 Cipolla, Wilma Reid. A
Catalog of   the Works of
Arthur William Foote, 1853-
1937. Detroit: Information
Coordinators, 1980.
     Lists all of the works by
genre and gives an annotation for each that includes
the location of the manuscript as well as performing
forces, publication information, dates of performances,
author of the text, etc.

030   Curtis, G.H.   "G. F.
Bristow."   Music,   3 (1893),
p. 547.
A biography of the com-
poser;   discusses   the oratorios Praise   to   God   and
Daniel   as   well   as The Pioneer,   in   addition   to the
opera Rip   Van Winkle and the
songs.   Includes a list of
works.

031   DeLerma, Dominique-
René.   Charles Edward Ives,
1874-1954: A Bibliography of
his Music.   Kent, Oh.: The
Kent State University Press,
1970.
Includes   all   of   Ives's
works,   giving   such information as title and alternate
titles   (when   they exist),
performance medium, publication information, and date of
composition.   The author has
also indexed the volume by
publication, by medium,   by
chronology, and by arranger,
poet,   librettist,   phono-
recordings and performer.

032 Drysdale, M. [Chadwick]
Hi Fidelity/Musical America,
27 (May, 1977), p. MA 20.
A review of a performance
of the composer's Judith by
Dartmouth College.   Includes
mention of possible influences on Chadwick and calls
for new recognition of the
composer.

033   Dwight, John Sullivan,
ed.   Dwight's Journal of
Music: A Paper of Art and
Literature.   Boston: Ditson,
1852-81.   Johnson Reprint

Corp., 1967.
Contains contemporary re-
views and articles of many
of these works included in
the present study as well as
biographical articles on the
composers.   Since these articles are too numerous to
include here, the reader is
referred to the separate index accompanying each volume of the Journal.

034   Ellinwood, Leonard.
The   History   of American
Church Music.   New   York:
Morehouse-Gorham Co., 1953.
Deals with most of the
composers in   this study.
The second section of the
book (pp. 65-130) is most
valuable, covering the period 1820-1920.   Appendix C
provides brief biographies
of the musicians.   Also
included in the book are
facsimiles of   Buck's The
Triumph of   David and L.
Mason's   Carmina Sacra, as
well as photos of Buck and
H. Parker.

035   Engel, Carl.   "Charles
Martin Loeffler."   Musical
Quarterly,   11   (1925),   p.
311.
A general article with
only brief mention of the
choral music, but includes a
good list of works.

036   Engel, Carl.   "George
W. Chadwick." Musical Quarterly, 10 (1924), p. 438.
Includes   an   excellent
list of works, but not very
valuable specifically con-

cerning the choral works.

Elijah.

037   Engen, David P.   "The Choral   Psalms   of Charles Ives: A Performer's Analysis of Psalm 90."   Church Music, No. 1 (1976), p. 20.
Gives a fairly detailed outline of the work, with suggestions for rehearsal procedure and performance practice. Includes a list of Ives's church and organ music.

038   Filbeck, Loren Harold. The Choral   Works   of Anthony Philip   Heinrich.   D.M.A. dissertation, University of Illinois, 1975.
Divides the choral works into four areas: hymns, small secular works, larger sacred and quasi-sacred pieces, and oratorios and cantatas. In-cludes those choruses in The Dawning of Music in Kentucky and The Sylviad. The disser-tation also contains the au-thors editions of The Jubilee and The Columbiad, as well as facsimile reproductions of Heinrich's published choral works.

039   Fiske, J.   "Music." Atlantic Monthly, 32 (August, 1873), p. 248.
Review   of   Paine's   St. Peter; also comments on Paine's Mass in D, comparing it to the Forty-Sixth Psalm of Dudley Buck and Whiting's Mass in C Minor. Includes a synopsis of St. Peter and a detailed comparison of the oratorio with Mendelssohn's

040   Foote, Arthur.   An Autobiography.   Norwood, Mass.: 1946.   Reprint with new introduction by Wilma Reid Cipolla, New York: Da Capo, 1979.
Includes comparisons of Foote's music to that of his contemporaries as well as memoirs and statements or information about several of the choral works. Also an index to the compositions. Cipolla's introduction pro-vides a brief biography of the composer as well as placing his life and work in the context of the nine-teenth century.

041   Gallo, William K.   The Life   and Church Music of Dudley Buck.   PhD. disser-tation, Catholic University of America, 1968.
Part One, Chapter Two is best for a discussion of the choral works. Part Two deals with stylistic elements in Buck's music.   There is a good list of works and a good bibliography as well as several illustrations and photos and numerous musical examples.

042   Graber, Kenneth. William Mason: An Annotated Bibliography.   To be pub-lished by: Detroit: Infor-mation Coordinators.
To include a catalog of works and a listing of writ-ings concerning Mason's piano pedagogy, theories,

and programs. Update of the author's dissertation on Mason.

043 Grantham, Donald. "A Harmonic Leitmotif System in Ives' 'Psalm 90.'" In Theory Only, 5 (May-June, 1979), p. 3.
A thorough analysis of the music, particularly with regard to the structural use of the five motives Ives uses at the opening of the work. Includes many musical examples.

044 Gray, Arlene Elizabeth. Lowell Mason's Contribution to American Church Music. Masters thesis, University of Rochester, 1941.
Deals primarily with Mason's contributions to hymnody but includes important chapters on Mason's advocacy of better church music with emphasis on choirs and their training.

045 Green, Douglas M. "Exempli gratia: a Chord Motive in Ives' 'Serenity'." In Theory Only, 4 (Oct. 1978), p. 20.
Discusses the importance of a B-diminished 9/7 chord and a C-sharp diminished seventh chord to Ives's composition, as well as the importance of the pitch class "A."

046 Groh, Jack Curran. A Conductor's Analysis of and Preparation and Approach to Polyrhythms: with Particu-

lar Attention to Polyrhythms in Certain of the Choral Works of Charles E. Ives. D.M.A. dissertation, University of Missouri-Kansas City, 1978.
Concentrates particularly on polyrhythmic activity in Three Harvest Home Chorales.

047 Hale, Philip. Charles Martin Loeffler. New York: G. Schirmer, n.d.
A publisher's catalog listing the works of Loeffler.

048 Harris, Carl Gordon Jr. A Study of Characteristic Stylistic Trends Found in the Choral Works of a Selected Group of Afro-American Composers and Arrangers. D.M.A. dissertation, University of Missouri-Kansas City, 1972.
Deals with the music of Work.

049 Harris, Roger. "Choral [concert review]." Music and Musicians, 27 (June 1979), p. 64.
Reviews a performance of Ives's The Celestial Country by Andrew Parrott and the Taverner Choir. Gives a short, but good analysis of the work as well as brief background information.

050 Henck, H. "Literatur zu Charles Ives." Neuland; Ansätze zur Musik der Gegenwart, 2 (1982-1983), p. 208.

051 Henck, H. "Literatur zu Charles Ives. Neuland; Ansätze zur Musik der Gegenwart, 3 (1983-84), p. 243.

052 Hill, R.S. "The Mysterious Chord of Henry Clay Work." Notes, 10 (1952-53), p. 211.
A rather long look at Work's career as a composer, concentrating primarily on the songs. It addresses not only his creative outlet but the question of why he has been unfairly neglected by history and quotes extensively from the composer's letters. Includes a good list of works.

053 Hitchcock, H. Wiley, and Perlis, Vivian. An Ives Celebration. Urbana, Ill.: University of Illinois Press, 1977.
Covers several topics, but most germane to this study is the essay by Nelly Bruce, "Ives and Nineteenth-Century American Music." (See 023)

054 Hitchcock, H. Wiley. Ives: A Survey of the Music. I.S.A.M. Monograph Number 19, New York: Brooklyn College (Institute for Studies in American Music), 1977.
Choral works are discussed individually on pp. 28-41. Provides a good overview of Ives's choral oeuvre.

055 Holl, Herbert. Some Versions of Pastoral in American Music. PhD. dissertation, University of Texas at Austin, 1980.
Discusses Root's The Haymakers and Phyllis, the Farmer's Daughter, and Heinrich's songs.

056 Howard, John Tasker. Our American Music, Three Hundred Years of It. New York: Thomas Y. Crowell Co., fourth ed., 1965.
Includes biographical material on most of the composers of this study but of most value is the chapter on church music which deals primarily with Buck and his successors.

057 Howe, Granville L. A Hundred Years of Music in America. Chicago: G.L. Howe, 1889.
An important and early history of American music. Chapters Four (on Lowell Mason), Six, Thirteen (on church music), and Twenty-one (on oratorio and dramatic works) are the most helpful. Includes information on all of the composers of this study.

058 Howe, M.A. DeWolfe. "John Knowles Paine." The Musical Quarterly, 25/3 (July, 1939), p. 257.
A discussion of Paine's background and years at Harvard, with mention of the Mass in D, and some anecdotal material on St. Peter, Oedipus, the Columbian March and Hymn, and other composi-

tions.

059 Hughes, Rupert. Contemporary American Composers,
being a Study of the Music of
this Country, its Present
Conditions and its Future,
with Critical Estimates and
Biographies of the Principal
Living Composers.... Boston:
Page, 1900; revised edition,
1914.
Includes basic material,
much of it gleaned from the
composers themselves, on
nearly everyone included in
my study.

060 Huxford, John Calvitt.
John Knowles Paine, his Life
and Works. PhD disserta-
tion, Florida State University, 1968.
Gives particular atten-
tion to large forms, especially the oratorios and
Mass. Gives a biography of
the composer and discusses
his contributions to American music and American music education.

061 Ives, Charles E.
Charles E. Ives: Memos. New
York: W.W. Norton, 1972.
Includes material of
Ives's on The Celestial
Country, his memories of
Parker and Chadwick, church
music, his own compilations
of his works, notes on Psalm
67, and a host of other
items. Also includes an in-
dex of names and an index of
Ives's music and writings.

062 Jacobs, Arthur, ed.
Choral Music. New York:
Penguin Books, 1963.
Chapter Ten: "After
Handel -- in Britain and
America," by Richard Franko
Goldman, and Chapter Twelve:
"The Oratorio and Cantata
Market," by Theodore M.
Finney, are most valuable.
Focuses primarily on the
major composers: L. Mason,
H. Parker, and so forth.

063 Jones, F.O. A Handbook
of American Music and
Musicians. New York: Da
Capo Press, 1971.
Brief biographical
sketches of most of the composers studied here. Each
entry, arranged alphabetically, ends with a short
list of works.

064 Jones, Maurice Allen.
American Theater Cantatas.
PhD dissertation, Univer-
sity of Illinois, 1975.
Examines twenty-five
"theater cantatas:" works
intended to be sung in concert or in staged produc-
tions that do not rely on
narration for continuity.
The period covered is 1852-
1907. Examines music by
Root (The Haymakers, Phyllis, the Farmer's Daughter)
as well as a comprehensive
listing of many other cantatas of this type. Jones
gives the author of the
text, performing forces, and
publication date.

065   Kauffman, Byron E.   The Choral Works of William Henry Fry.   D.M.A.   dissertation, University of Illinois, 1975.

Examines the four principal choral works of Fry: Hallelujah Chorus, Ode (for the New York Crystal Palace), Stabat Mater, and Mass in E-flat.   The dissertation also provides modern performing editions of each work.

066   Kearns, William Kay. Horatio Parker: A Bio-Bibliographical Study. (to be published in the College Music Society Bibliographies in American Music Series).

Will provide a list of Parker's music with the location of the manuscript and information on the first performance of each work. Also will include a bibliography of writings by Parker and about him and his works.

067   Kearns, William Kay. Horatio Parker, 1863-1919: A Study of his Life and Music. PhD dissertation, University of Illinois, 1965.

There are sections on Parker's partsongs, cantatas, ceremonial music, major choral works, and church music. Also includes analysis of some of the compositions. There is also very good information concerning Parker's relationships with various choral societies.

068   Keats, S. "Reference Articles on American Composers; An Index." Juil-liard Review, 1 (Fall, 1953), p. 30.

069   Kent, Ralph McVety. A Study of Oratorios and Sacred Cantatas Composed in America before 1900. PhD dissertation, University of Iowa, 1954.

Represents the first attempt at gathering material on the major works of this period.   Examines 71 works by 26 composers. Part One is a résumé of the development of music in America. Part Two consists of biographies of the composers and analyses of their works, as well as photoreproductions of the composer's manuscripts.   Also includes several appendixes and a lengthy bibliography.   The works included: Root: Daniel, David, the Shepherd Boy, Under the Palms, The Choicest Gift, Faith Triumphant, Belshazzar's Feast, The Building of the Temple Florens (subtitled The Pilgrim, or The Children of the Plain), Jacob and Esau, and Star of Light; Bradbury: Daniel, Esther; Buck: Easter Morning, The Forty-sixth Psalm, The Nun of Nidaros, The Story of the Night, The Story of the Cross, The Triumph of David, The Coming of the King; Paine: Mass in D, St. Peter; J.C.D. Parker: Redemption Hymn, St. John, Psalm 137; Gilchrist: Prayer and Praise; Chadwick: Dedication Ode, The Pilgrims, Judith, Noel; H. Parker: Hora Novissima, The Holy Child, The Legend of

St. Christopher, Adstant
angelorum chori, The Shepherd's Vision.

070 Kenyon, Nicholas. "Fur-
ther Events." The New York-
er, 56 (June 21, 1982), p.
107.
Review of Beach's Mass in
E-flat at the Church of the
Ascension in New York. Discusses orchestration and
style, and the Mass's appeal
to modern concert audiences;
compares the composer to
Rossini.

071 Kirkpatrick, John.
"Charles E. Ives: Harvest
Home Chorales." Notes, 6
(June, 1949), p. 486.
Review of the works,
including suggestions for
making performance of the
rhythms easier.

072 Kirkpatrick, John. Temporary Catalog of Music Mss.
of Charles E. Ives. New Hav-
en: Yale University Press,
1960.
A description of all the
manuscripts given to Yale by
the composer's wife. The
catalog is divided into seven
parts categorized by performing medium and includes mul-
tiple indexes to such items
as titles, dedications, music
paper used, tunes quoted,
publishers, etc.

073 Kumlien, Wendell C.
"The Music for Chorus."
Music Educators Journal, 61
(Oct. 1974), p. 48.

The author gives a brief
description of each of
Ives's choral works, including date of composition,
publication data (if appli-
cable), and a note about
texture or a unique feature
of the work.

074 Kumlien, Wendell C.
The Sacred Choral Music of
Charles Ives: A Study in
Style Developments. PhD
dissertation, University of
Illinois, 1969.
Involves a detailed dis-
cussion of 23 sacred choral
works. Includes an exam-
ination of the sources for
study, factors conditioning
Ives's choice of texts, and
a summary/conclusion sec-
tion. Also lists all of the
sacred works available ei-
ther published or in mss.
Appendix One has transcrip-
tions of 18 unpublished
works with their manuscript
sources reproduced in Ap-
pendix Two.

075 Lamb, Gordon H. "In-
terview with Robert Shaw (on
the Music of Charles Ives)."
The Choral Journal, 15/8
(1975), p. 5.
Shaw discusses how he
came to perform Ives's music
as well as how he solved rehearsal problems in many of
the works.

076 Lang, Paul Henry, ed.
One Hundred Years of Music
in America. G. Schirmer,
1961.
- Chapter Five: "Church Mu-

sic: A   Century   of   Contrasts," by Robert Stevenson. (See **115**).

077   Ledbetter,   Steven.
George   W.   Chadwick (1854–
1931):   A   Bibliographical
Source-Book, 1983.   Type-
script.   Available at the New
England Conservatory of Music, Boston.
   An excellent source for
information   concerning
Chadwick's choral music. Not
only lists basic compositional and publication data but
often has additional information,   including comments
from reviews, letters, etc.
dealing with a specific work.

078   Lowens,   Margery M.
MacDowell.   (To be published
by: Detroit: Information
Coordinators).
   International in scope,
covering periods 1879–1980 or
so.   To   include published
sources by   and about the
composer,   letters and mss.
sources,   with their loca-
tions, and a discography.

079 Lowens, Margery M. The
New York Years of Edward
MacDowell.   PhD dissertation, University of Michigan, 1971.
   A   general   biography
covering   the   years 1896–
1908,   with   an   important
appendix: a   listing   of
MacDowell's music with the
dates   of   composition and
publication and the location
of the mss., intended as a
supplement   to   Sonneck's

Catalog of First Editions
(See **112**).

080   Maisel,   Edward M.
Charles T. Griffes.   New
York: Knopf, 1984.
   The choral works are discussed in the context of the
composer's life in this biography.   There is also a
list of works divided be-
tween   published and unpublished compositions and a
complete index.

081 Mason, Daniel Gregory.
"Arthur Whiting."   The Musical Quarterly, 23 (Jan.
1937), p. 26.
   A brief biography of the
composer in the form of a
memoir,   quoting liberally
from   Whiting's essays on
music.   Examines influences
upon the composer.

082 Mason, Daniel Gregory.
Music in My Time. New York:
MacMillan, 1938.
   Begins with an autobiography and continues with
reminiscences of W. Mason
and   A.B.   Whiting,   with
photos of both. The book is
a good source for general
biography, included here because of scarcity of material on Whiting and on Mason
himself.

083   Mason, Henry Lowell.
Lowell Mason: an Appre-
ciation of his Life and
Work. New York, 1941.

084   Mason,   William.   Mem-
ories of a Musical Life.   New
York: Century Company, 1901.
Reprint: New   York: AMS
Press;   Reprint: New York:
Da   Capo   Press,   1970.
Contains   information   on
Heinrich as well as photos of
W. Mason and a brief auto-
biography   of   his   life with
his father Lowell.   The Ap-
pendix   is   entitled   "Early
Life of Lowell Mason" and
includes a photo. Examines
influences   on   L.   Mason's
life.

085 Matthews, W.S.B.   "German Influence upon American
Music as Noted in the Work of
Dudley   Buck,   J.K.   Paine,
William Mason, J.C.D. Parker,
and Stephen A. Emery." The
Musician, 15 (1910), p. 160.
A very interesting article
drawing upon the choral works
of these   composers to illus-
trate   the   article's   main
points, in particular Paine's
St. Peter and Buck's Te Deum.

086 Matthews, W.S.B., ed.   A
Hundred Years of Music in
America. Chicago: G.L. Howe,
1889.
Several chapters are relevant: Chapter Four, on L.
Mason; Chapter Six, "Progress
of Oratorio to 1840;"   Chapter   Thirteen,   "Liturgical
Music;" and Chapter Twenty-
one,   "Dramatic,   orchestral
and   oratorio   composers."
Includes many illustrations
and   photos.   Covers almost
all of the composers in this
study.

087 McKinley, Ann.   "Music
for   the   Dedication Ceremonies of the World's Columbian Exposition in Chicago." American Music.   3/1
(1985), p. 42.
Deals with the circum-
stances surrounding Paine's
Columbus March and Hymn and
Chadwick's   Ode.   Includes
photos of the dedication
ceremonies, and a good bibliography and notes section.

088   Merrill, E. Lindsay.
Mrs. H.H.A. Beach: her Life
and Music.   PhD dissertation, University of Rochester, 1963.
Divides the vocal music
into three categories based
on musical style.   Most of
the dissertation is general
in nature, but does discuss
the choral works within the
context of the composers
life.

089   Miller, John. Edward
MacDowell: A   Critical
Study.   PhD dissertation,
University of Rochester,
1961.

090   Moore, Alicia Y. A
Study of Anthony Philip
Heinrich, an American Com-
poser. Masters thesis, Uni-
versity of North Carolina-
Greensboro, 1963.

091   New   York.   Columbia
University Library.   Cat-
alogue of an Exhibition Il-
lustrating the Life and Work
of Edward MacDowell, 1861-

1908,. . .Together with the
Addresses Delivered at the
Opening Ceremonies, April 27,
1938. New York: 1938.
Includes descriptions of
several autograph scores and
a facsimile of Op. 27, the
Drei Lieder für vierstimmigen
Männerchor.

092 Ogasapian, J.K. "Lowell
Mason as a Church Musician."
Journal of Church Music, 21
(September, 1979), p. 6
An article that discusses
Lowell Mason's background and
experience as a church musician, giving particular attention to his collection of
hymns and church pieces. May
be helpful to the choral conductor for its information on
performance practice.

093 Osgood, G.L. "St. Peter, an Oratorio." North
American Review, 117 (1873),
p. 247.
Review of Paine's ora-
torio. Includes some theoretical analysis as well as
comments on the background of
the work, its text, and a
prediction of its place in
music history.

094 Paige, Paul Eric. Musical Organizations in Boston:
1830-1850. PhD dissertation,
Boston University, 1967.
Studied fourteen major
choral and instrumental organizations in Boston. Concludes that choral music dom-
inated the Boston musical
scene in this time period.
Discusses Lowell Masons's

role in the musical life of
the city as well as that
role played by church
choirs.

095 Porte, John F. Edward
MacDowell (A Great American
Tone Poet, His Life and Music). London: Keagan, Paul,
Trench, Trubner and Co.,
1922.
Begins with a biograph-
ical sketch followed by
chapters on MacDowell as a
man and a composer, including a short chapter on the
MacDowell Colony. The bulk
of the book is devoted to a
description of each of Mac-
Dowell's works (including
those without opus numbers)
and ends with an alphabet-
ical index to the works.

096 Roberts, Kenneth C.,
Jr. John Knowles Paine.
PhD dissertation, University
of Michigan, 1962.

097 Rogers, Delmar Dalnell.
Nineteenth-century Music in
New York City as Reflected
in the Career of G.F.
Bristow. Masters thesis,
University of Michigan,
1967.
Examines Bristow's role
as conductor of church and
city choral groups. In-
cludes analysis of his works
by genre.

098 Root, G.F. The Story
of a Musical Life. Cin-
cinnati: John Church Co.,
1981. Reprint: New York:

Da Capo Press, 1970.

Includes important information, especially on his career as a church musician and a great deal of his choral works, among them: Pillar of Fire, The Haymakers and other cantatas. The Appendix lists his publications (writings and songs). The book also includes scores to several musical works: Slumber Sweetly, Dearest by William Mason, and Root's own A Voice from the Lake, There is a Stream, The Shining Shore, and I will Lay Me Down in Sleep for mixed voices, and There's Music in the Air for men's voices.

099 Rorick, W.C. "The Horatio Parker Archives in the Yale University Music Library." Fontes Artes Musicae, 26 (1979), p. 298.

An annotated bibliography of letters, papers, correspondence, etc. of the composer. Over 400 items, arranged chronologically and then by subject.

100 Salter, Sumner. "Early Encouragement to American Composers." The Musical Quarterly, 18 (1932), p. 76.

Some very interesting material concerning the American Composer's Choral Association (fl. 1877-88) and its performances of Buck's Light of Asia; MacDowell's King Ring's Death, Burial and Apotheosis [N.B.: not included in any list of the composer's works] as well as his Barcarolle; Chadwick's Lovely Rosabelle; and Foote's Wreck of the Hesperus.

101 Scher, Paula Vandenberg. Charles Ives: An Annotated Bibliography for 1970-1975. City University of New York, Graduate School Library, New York City.

Includes only significant articles in English from periodicals listed in the Music Article Guide and Music Index, categorized by biography, style, technique, and genre of composition.

102 Schleifer, Martha Furman. William Wallace Gilchrist: Life and Work. PhD dissertation, Bryn Mawr College, 1976.

Divided into two parts, "Life" and "Works." Includes a thematic catalog for all the choral works and also includes scores for two of the choral works: To Song, and The Forty-sixth Psalm in the appendixes.

103 Schleifer, Martha Furman. "William Wallace Gilchrist, Philadelphia Musician." Diapason, 72 (May, 1981), p. 1.

Gives a short but very good biography of Gilchrist including his work with the Mendelssohn Club of Philadelphia. The choral works get little space, though there are several good paragraphs on his compositional technic.

104 Schleifer, Martha Furman. _William Wallace Gilchrist (1846-1916): A Moving Force in the Musical Life of Philadelphia_. Metuchen, N.J.: Scarecrow Press, 1985.

A thematic catalog of the choral works, separated sacred and secular, appears on pp. 88-130. Includes a good listing of bibliographical material in the section marked "Sources consulted."

105 Schmidt, John C. _The Life and Works of John Knowles Paine_. PhD dissertation, New York University, 1979. Ann Arbor: UMI Research Press, 1980.

Examines the _Mass in D_, _St. Peter_, the music to _Oedipus Tyrannus_, as well as smaller works. Includes a list of works. The second section of the dissertation is an analytical and descriptive survey of all the compositions, including the location of the manuscript, publication history, performance history, and an analysis of each work. In the book, the choral music is covered on pp. 411-558.

106 Semler, Isabel Parker. _Horatio Parker: A Memoir for his Grandchildren_. New York: G.P. Putnam, 1942. Reprint: New York: Da Capo Press, 1973.

Primarily a biography of the composer, the book also contains a list of works and many photos and illustrations, including a facsimile of the first page of _Hora novissima_.

107 Smith, David Stanley. "A Study of Horatio Parker." _The Musical Quarterly_, 16 (1930), p. 153.

A brief biography of the composer. Includes a facsimile of the first page of _Hora novissima_.

108 Smith, Elizabeth E. _A Study of Canticum fratris solis by Charles Martin Loeffler_. Masters thesis, University of Rochester, 1947.

109 Smith, Gregg. "Charles Ives and his Music for Chorus." _The Choral Journal_, 15/3 (1974), p. 17.

Smith gives a good background on Ives's life and the importance of his compositions, focusing on the choral works. He includes a list of the choral works and publication data for them when available.

110 Snyder, L. "Musical 'Wrecks' from the Past Onstage." _Christian Science Monitor_, 64 (Aug. 10, 1972), p. 4.

Review of the Foote's _Wreck of the Hesperus_ in Newport, R.I.

111 Sole, Kenneth Gale. _A Study and Performance of Five Psalm Settings and "The_

Celestial Country" by Charles
Edward   Ives.   D.M.A.
dissertation, University of
Southern California, 1976.
Examines Ives's settings
of psalms 14, 67, 90, 100,
150 and The Celestial Country
in detail.

112   Sonneck, O.G.   Cata-
logue of First Editions of
Edward MacDowell. Washington: Government Printing Office, 1917.
Arranged in five sections:
works   with   opus numbers;
works without opus numbers;
works   written   under   the
pseudonyms Edgar Thorn and
Thorne; partsongs and orchestra   music   edited;   and
piano works   edited.   There
are also six indexes to the
volume.

113   Starr, L.   "Charles
Ives: the Next Hundred Years,
Towards a Method of Analyzing
the Music."   Music Review,
38/2 (1977), p. 101.
An important article that
deals with elements of Ives's
style that may become even
more important as we gain
historical perspective on his
works.

114   "The Early Styles of
Charles   Ives.   Nineteenth-
Century Music, 7/1 (1983), p.
71.
Divides   Ives's   early
styles into   several   "man-
ners:"   conservative, radi-
cal, and a third category
called "diversity and co-
herence." Examines Psalms 54

and 67, The Celestial Country, as well as the song
"Feldeinsamkeit."

115   Stevenson, Robert.
"Church Music: A Century of
Contrasts." in One Hundred
Years of Music in America,
Paul Henry Lang, ed. New
York: G. Schirmer, 1961, p.
80.
Mentions   the   contribu-
tions of Chadwick, Paine, H.
Parker, Ives, Buck, J.C.D.
Parker and others, and dis-
cusses many major works of
these composers.

116   Stevenson, Robert.
Protestant   Church   Music in
America.   New York: W.W.
Norton, 1966, p. 81.
Chapters Eight and Ten
are pertinent to this study,
citing the composers L. Mason, Bradbury, Buck, Paine,
and H. Parker.

117   Strunk, W. Oliver.
"Works of Horatio Parker."
The Musical Quarterly, 16/2
(April, 1930), p. 164.
A complete list of works,
with publication data, com-
piled as a companion article
to the piece on Parker by
David   Stanley Smith (see
107).

118   Taylor, Jewel Anna-
belle. Technical Practices
of Negro Composers in Choral
Works for A Cappella Choir.
Masters thesis, University
of Rochester, 1960.
Examines   the   music   of

Henry Clay Work.

119 Tipton, J.R. "Some Observations on the Choral Style of Charles Ives." American Choral Review, 12/3 (1970), p. 99.

Compares Psalm 24 and the Three Harvest Home Chorales, including rather in-depth analyses of both works in terms of structure, melodic technique, harmonic techniques, etc. Includes several musical examples.

120 Tuthill, Burnet C. "Mrs H.H.A. Beach." The Musical Quarterly, 26 (1940), p. 297.

The article is mainly a biography of the composer but also discusses stylistic elements of her works. The article includes a list of works, a photo, and a facsimile of Christ in the Universe.

121 Ulrich, Homer. A Survey of Choral Music. New York: Harcourt Brace Jovanovich, 1973.

Parker's Hora novissima is covered briefly on p. 176.

122 Upton, George Putnam. The Standard Cantatas: Their Stories, Their Music, and Their Composers, A Handbook. Chicago: A.C. McClurg, 1889.

Begins with a short history of the cantata and then examines the following works: Buck: Don Munio, The Centennial Meditation, The Golden Legend, The Voyage of Columbus, The Light of Asia; Foote: Hiawatha; Gilchrist: The Forty-sixth Psalm; Paine: Oedipus Tyrannus, The Nativity, The Realm of Fancy, Phoebus, Arise; H. Parker: King Trojan; J.C.D. Parker: The Redemption Hymn; G.E. Whiting: The Tale of the Viking. Each entry has a short biographical sketch of the composer followed by a description/synopsis of the work cited.

123 Upton, George Putnam. The Standard Oratorios: Their Stories, Their Music, and Their Composers, A Handbook. Chicago: A.C. McClurg, 1886.

Begins with a short history of the oratorio and then examines a number of works, including Paine's St. Peter. Concludes with a chapter entitled "Sacred Music in America," which is historical in nature.

124 Upton, William Treat. Anthony Philip Heinrich: A Nineteenth-Century Composer in America. New York: Columbia University Press, 1939.

The main body of the work is a biography of the composer. The appendixes discuss various topics, including separate sections dealing with The Dawning of Music in Kentucky and The Western Minstrel. There follows a list of compositions in the Musid Division of the Library of Congress.

125   Upton, William Treat.
The Musical Works of William
Henry Fry in the   Collection
of The Library Company of
Philadelphia.   Philadelphia:
Free Library of Philadelphia,
1946.
    Printed as an appendix to
Upton's biography of the com-
poser (see 126).

126   Upton, William Treat.
William Henry Fry: American
Journalist   and   Composer-
Critic. New York: Thomas Y.
Crowell Co., 1954. Reprint:
Da Capo Press, 1974.
    Discusses the choral works
in the main body of the text,
which is a chronological ac-
count of the composer's life.
Includes a list of works in
the Library Company of Philadelphia by genre and a good
index to works discussed in
the text. Does not include a
bibliography.

127   Van Camp, Leonard.
"Nineteenth-century   Choral
Music in America: A German
Legacy."   American   Choral
Review, 23/4 (1981), p. 5
    Mentions the   following
composers and works: Paine:
(St. Peter, Mass in D;) H.
Parker: (Hora novissima);
Chadwick, and Ives. Best as
a source of background ma-
terial for these works.

128   Vinquist, Mary. The
Psalm Settings of Charles
Ives.   Masters thesis, Indi-
ana University, 1965.

129 Walker, Donald R.   "The
Vocal   Music   of   Charles
Ives." Parnassus, 3/2 (Summer, 1975), p. 329.
    Discusses the vocal and
choral works of Ives. Choral works included are: Celestial   Country,   all the
psalm settings, New River,
and others. Good for placing these works within a
context of Ives's other vocal writings.

130   Washington, D.C. Library of Congress. Music
Division. [Heinrich].
    Scrapbook containing the
composer's   manuscripts as
well as other material.

131   Wells,   W.B.   "Sacred
Choral   Octavos."   Notes,
30/3 (1974), p. 634.
    Compares   and   reviews
Ives's Three Harvest Home
Chorales,   The   Celestial
Country, Psalm 90, Psalm 67,
Psalm 135,   Psalm 24, and
Psalm 25.

132   Wiig, John.   An Analysis of Transcendental Influences in Selected Choral
Works of Charles Ives. Masters thesis, Mankato State
University, 1972.
    Examines   transcendental
influences on Ives's compositional techniques in three
segments: melody, rhythm,
and harmony.   Then analyzes
Psalm 67, Psalm 24, and the
Three Harvest Home Chorales.

133 Woodward, Henry. "Processional: Let There Be Light." Notes, 13 (March, 1956), p. 349.
A very brief review of Ives's work.

134 Young, Percy. The Choral Tradition. New York: W. W. Norton, 1981.
Chapter Six: "The Nineteenth Century II," provides limited information of the larger choral works of Buck, Paine, Chadwick, Foote, H. Parker, and Ives.

INDEXES

INDEX A1:   WORKS FOR MIXED OR UNISON VOICES WITH ORCHESTRA

A.D. 1919 (1020)
Adieu, The (0797)
Admiral of the Seas, The (0692)
Agnus Dei (0693)
Allegory of War and Peace, An (1023)
America to France (0695)
Ave Maria (0149)

Ballade (1028)
Bedouin Song (0429)
Belshazzar (0699)
Belshazzar's Feast (1205)
Bethlehem (1206)

Canticle of the Sun, The (0014)
Celestial Country, The (0842)
Centennial Hymn (0996)
Centennial Meditation of Columbia (0169)
Christ in the Universe (0016)
Christmas Idyll, A (0571)
Circus Band (0844)
Columbia (0314)
Columbiad, The (0802)
Coro funerale (0803)

Daniel (0124)
De profunsis (0578)
Dedication Ode (0320)
Divine Tragedy (0713)
Dream-King and His Love (1046)
Dream of Mary (1047)
Dream Picture (1256)

Easter Anthem: Christ Our Passover (0714)
Easter Idyll, An (0582)
Easter Morning (0186)
Election, An (0849)
Esther, the Beautiful Queen (0107)

Fairies, The (0717)
Faith Triumphant (1212)
Felsen von Plymouth, Die (0811)
Festival Te Deum in C (1259)
Festival Jubilate (0030)
Flower Queen, The (1215)
Forty-sixth Psalm, The (0200)
Freedom Our Queen (0999)

General Booth (0852)
Great Republic, The: Ode to the American Union (0128)

Hallelujah Chorus (0537)
Harold Harfager (1061)
He is There! (0857)
Hora novissima (1065)
Hymn of the West (1003)

Idylle (1073)
In Arcady (0738)
In Music's Praise (0739)

Jabberwocky (0743)
Jacob and Esau (1219)

Jerusalem (0418)
Jubilee, The (0817)
Judith (0344)

King Gorm the Grim (1081)
Kobolds, The (1084)
König Trojan (1085)
Kyrie eleison (0538)

Land of Our Hearts (0346)
Laus artium (1087)
Legend of Don Munio, The
    (0232)
Legend of St. Christopher,
    The (1089)
Lelawala: A Legend of
    Niagara (0750)
Leonora (1268)
Life of Man, The (1185)
Light of Asia (0233)
Lily Nymph, The (0349)
Lincoln, the Great Commoner
    (0863)
Lord God Omnipotent, The
    (0540)
Lovely Rosabelle (0353)

Majority (The Masses) (0866)
Mass in C (0132)
Mass in C Minor (1271, 1272)
Mass in D (1004)
Mass in E-flat (0051, 0541)
May Day (0754)
Merlin and Vivian (0755)
Midnight (1274)
Mirtil in Arcadia (0756)
Morven and the Grail (1099)
Moses in Egypt (0542)
Music: An Ode (0757)
Musings of the Wild Wood
    (0822)

Nativity, The (1006)
New Earth, The (0762)
New River, The (0869)
Niagara (0135, 0823)

Ninetieth Psalm, The (0631)
Noël (0365)

O santa Maria (0825)
Ode (0543)
Ode for the Opening of the
    Chicago World's Fair,
    (0371)
Ode Written for G. S., No.
    20 (0137)

Philadelphia Historical
    Pageant (0421)
Phoenix Expirans (0374)
Phyllis, the Farmer's
    Daughter (1220)
Pilgrims, The (0375)
Pioneer, The (0140)
Praise to God (0141)
Prayer and Praise (0642)
Prophecy and Fulfillment
    (0775)
Psalm 46 (0643)
Psalm 137 (1187)

Realm of Fancy, The (1012)
Redemption Hymn (1188)
Resurgam (0777)
Rose, The (0648)

St. John (1190)
St. Peter (1013)
Scenes from the Golden
    Legend (0262)
Semper vivrens (0783)
Skeleton in Armor, The
    (0512)
Song of Promise (1017)
Song of Times, A (1136)
Song of Welcome (0079)
Stabat Mater (0544)
Star Song, A (1139)
Story of the Cross, The
    (0275)
Sylvania (0080)
Sylviador, The (0832)

Tale of the Viking, The (1280)

They Are There! (0888)

Under the Palms (1225)

Union and Liberty (1156)

Viking's Last Voyage, The (0409)

Walt Whitman (0891)

Wanderer's Psalm, A (1159)

Wreck of the Hesperus, The (0534)

INDEX A2:   WORKS FOR MIXED OR UNISON VOICES
WITH SMALL ENSEMBLE OR KEYBOARD ACCOMPANIMENT

Come O'er the Sea (0573)
Come See the Place (1043)
Come See the Place Where Jesus Lay (0574)
Come Unto Me (0316)
Coming of the King, The (0178)
Commemoration Ode (0317)
Communion Service (0845)
Constant Christmas (0022)
Crossing the Bar (0846)

Daniel (1210)
David, The Shepherd Boy (1211)
Day Gently Sinking, The (0576)
Day is Past and Over, The (0577)
Desert Shall Rejoice, The (1227)
Deus misereatur in E (1045)
Deus misereatur in A (1176)
Does the Road Wind Uphill All the Way? (0444)

Easter Anthem (0125)
Easter Anthem in E-flat (1177)
Easter Anthem in G (1178)
Easter Anthem in A (1179)
Easter Anthem in B-flat (0186)
Easter Carol (0848)
Ecclesia (1048)
Elegiac quintetto vocale (0806)
Emmanuel (0583)
Epitaph on Joan Bugg (0807)
Evening (0327)
Evening Hymn (0027, 0189)
Evening Service (0190, 0191, 0192)
Evening Service in D (0126)
Except the Lord Build the House (0584)
Far from the World (1049)
Father of All (0585)

Fathers of the Free (0328)
Festival Hymn (0193)
Festival Morning Service (0194)
Festival Te Deum and Jubilate (0197)
Fill Your Goblets (0812)
Five Settings of the Venite, exultemus Domino (1228)
Flag, The (0721)
Fountain, The (0722)
Four Partsongs (0723)
Funeral Anthem (0813)
Future, The (0587)

Gettysburg Address (0724)
Give Ear, O Shepherd of Israel (1229)
Give Unto the Lord (1055)
Give Unto the Lord, O Ye Mighty (0201)
God is My Strong Salvation (0590)
God Is Our Refuge and Strength (0450)
God of Abraham Praise, The (0207)
God of My Life (0854)
God that Made Earth and Heaven (0592)
God that Makest Earth and Heaven (1057)
God Who Madest Earth and Heaven (0209)
Good Morrow (1262)
Gracious Is the Lord (1230)

Hail Beauteous Spring (0816)
Hark! Hark! My Soul (0215)
Hark, What Mean Those Holy Voices (0593, 1231)
Haymakers, The (1217)
He Faileth Not (1062)
He Shall Come Down Like Rain (0217)
He that Dwelleth in the Secret Place (0728)
He Who Hath Led Will Lead

(1063)
Hearken Unto Me (0034)
Hide Me O Twilight Air (0594)
His Salvation Is Nigh (1232)
Holy Child, The (1064)
Home They Brought Her Warrior
  Dead (0595)
Hong Kong Romance, A (0731)
How Long Wilt Thou Forget Me,
  O Lord? (0596)
How   Silent,   How   Spacious
  (0735)
Hymn for Easter (1264)
Hymn of Freedom, A (0036)
Hymn of the Pilgrim (0926)

I Cannot Find Thee (0457)
I Heard the Voice of Jesus
  Say (0598)
I Love the Lord (0600)
I Shall Not Die but Live
  (1070, 1234)
I Will Call Upon Thee (0220)
I Will Give Thanks (0038)
I Will Lift Up Mine Eyes
  (0221)
If Thou But Suffer God to
  Guide Thee (0461, 0462)
If Ye Then Be Rich with
  Christ (0602)
Immortal, The (0334, 0737)
Irish Folk Song, An (0469)
It Came Upon a Midnight Clear
  (0605)

Jesus, I My Cross Have Taken
  (0606)
Jesus,   Lover   of   My Soul
  (0607)
Jesus, the Very Thought of
  Thee (0608)
Joyful Morn, The (0744)
Jubilate in D (1181)
Jubilate in E (1182, 1183)
Jubilate in G (1184)
Jubilate in A-flat (0472)
Jubilate in B-flat (0343)
Jubilate Deo (0229)

Jubilee Hymn (1080)
June (0043)
Just As I Am (0615)

Lamb of God, The (0617)
Laurel's Twined Around the
  Warrior's Brow (0539)
Law of the Lord Is Perfect
  (0474)
Let This Mind Be in You
  (0045)
Let Us Rise Up and Build
  (1090)
Light that Is Felt, The
  (0862)
Light's   Glittering   Morn
  (1091)
Listen, O Isles, Unto Me
  (0476)
Little Lac Grenier (0350)
Lord God, Thy Sea is Mighty
  (0864)
Lord Is in His Holy Temple
  (0969)
Lord Is King, The (0235)
Lord Is My Light, The (1093)
Lord Is My Strength and
  Song, The (0751)
Lord of All Power and Might
  (0351)
Lord of the Worlds Above
  (0049, 0479)
Lord Reigneth, The (0620)
Lord, Thou Hast Searched Me
  (1237)
Lord's Prayer, The (0481)

Magnificat in E-flat (1096)
Magnificat   in   G   Major
  (Festival) (0625)
Magnificat and Nunc dimittis
  in E-flat (1097)
Magnificat and Nunc dimittis
  in B-flat (0486)
Mass in F Minor (1273)
May Carol, A (0358)
May Eve (0052)
Mexican Serenade (0359)

(0520)
Sentences   and   Responses
  (0387)
Serenity (0885)
Service in A (0074)
Seven Partsongs (1193)
Shadows of the Evening Hours
  (0654)
Shed No Tear! (1278)
Shena Van (0075)
Shepherd's Vision, The (1130)
Shine! Shine! (0655)
Short Te Deum and Benedictus
  (0264)
Sing Hosanna in the Highest
  (0266)
Sing, O Sing, This Blessed
  Morn (0658)
Sing We Alleluia (0659)
Sinner Turn, Why Will Ye Die?
  (0660)
Sirens, The (1279)
Six Anthems (1131)
Sneak Thief (0886)
Song of the Night, The (0272)
Song Tournament, The (1223)
Star of Light, The (1224)
Still, Still With Thee (0516)

Te Deum in C (1194)
Te Deum in D (0517, 1195)
Te Deum in E-flat (1196)
Te Deum in E (1142, 1197,
  1198)
Te Deum in F (1199)
Te Deum in G (1200)
Te Deum in A (1143, 1201)
Te   Deum   in   B   Minor   and
  Benedictus   in   E   Major
  (0284)
Te   Deum   in   B-flat   (0518,
  1202)
Te   Deum   and   Jubilate   in   C
  (0279)
Te   Deum   and   Jubilate   in   E-
  flat   (0519)
Te Deum laudamus in B-flat
  (1144)
Te Dominum in F (0679)

Thanks Be to God (0520)
There   is   a   Land   of   Pure
  Delight (1145)
There   Was   a   Little   Man
  (0787)
There Was Darkness (0285)
There Were Shepherds (0788)
These Things Shall Be (0691)
They That Wait Upon the Lord
  (1243)
Thou   Art   Fairer   than   the
  Children of Man (1244)
Thou Knowest, Lord (0084)
Thou Shalt Remember (1147)
Thou   Wilt   Keep   Him   in
  Perfect Peace (0286)
Three Anthems (0287)
Three   Sacred   Quartettes
  (0405)
Three   Harvest Home Chorales
  (0889)
Thy Way, Not Mine (0523)
To Song (0681)
Tribute, The: The   City of
  Fraternal Love (0833)
Triumph of David, The (0288)
Triumphal March (1154)
Turn Ye, Turn Ye (0890)
Two Anthems (0793)

Uplifted Gates, The (0682)

Venite in C (0528)
Vesperal Psalms, The (1283)
Vespers   of   the   Blessed
  Virgin (1284)

Watchman   Tell   Us   of   the
  Night (0985)
We Who Sing (0090)
Weary of Earth (0683)
Western   Minstrel's   Musical
  Compliments   to   Mrs.
  Coutts, The (0835)
What E'er My God Ordains is
  Right (0684)
What Say? (0411)

When the Lord Turned Again
    the Captivity of Zion
    (0295)
When the Weary Seeking Rest
    (0686)
While Shepherds Watched
    (0415)
Who Shall Roll Us Away the

Stone? (1163)
World's Wanderers, The
    (1204)
Winds, The (1286)

Year's At the Spring, The
    (0096)

INDEX A3:   WORKS FOR UNACCOMPANIED MIXED OR UNISON VOICES

Saviour, Like a Shepherd (0386)
Sentence (0979)
Serenade (0884, 0993)
Shine! Shine! (0655)
Shout the Glad Tidings (0656)
Shout, Ye High Heavens (0389)
Song of Farewell (0980)
Song of the Flag (0271)
Songs Prepared for...Fourth of July (0981)
Sweet Rivers (0114)

Te Deum in F (0082)
Teach Me, O Lord (0396)
Thanksgiving Anthem (0982)
There Were Shepherds (0397)
Thou Shalt Love the Lord the God (0400)
Thou Who Art Love Divine (0401)
Three Patriotic Songs (0983)

Three Poems by Shakespeare (0789)
Three Sacred Anthems (0404)
Three School Songs (0086)
Thrushes (0790)
Trust in God (0115)
Two Northern Songs (0944)
Two Sanctuses and Anthems (0984)

Vesper Hymns, The (1282)
Vita nostra plena bellis (0529)
Voice that Breathed O'er Eden, The (1158)

War Song (0949)
Welcome Happy Morn (0410)
When Spring Is Calling (0994)
While Thee I Seek (0416)
Who Has Seen the Wind (0054)

Year's at the Spring, The (0892)

INDEX A4: WORKS FOR WOMEN'S VOICES

This Morning Very Early (0083)
Three Choruses (0402)
Three Flower Songs (0085)
Three Shakespeare Songs (0086)
Three Songs (0088)
Three Summer Songs (0680)
Through the House Give Glimmering Light (0089)
Through the Rushes, by the River (0522)
Thy Beaming Eyes (0942)
Time of Parting, The (0791)
To Daffodils (0524)
Toll of the Sea, The (0792)
Tomorrow (0525)

Two Four-Part Choruses (0407, 0408)

What Is More Gentle (0685)
What the Winds Bring (0796)
When I View the Mother Holding (0412)
Where Shall I Find a White Rose Blowing (0531)
While We Have Time (1161)
Wouldn't That Be Queer? (0093)

Year's At the Spring, The (0094, 0095)

INDEX A5: WORKS FOR MEN'S VOICES

(0509)
Serenade (0388, 1242)
Shena Van (0076)
Sing Alleluia Forth (0265)
Six Songs for Male Voices
 (0268)
Soldier's Oath (1016)
Song of April, A (0515)
Song of Mary's, A (0887)
Song of the Drum, The (0270)
Song of the Sea (0785)
Song of the Viking (0391)
Spirit of Beauty (1137)
Summer Night, A (0276)
Summer Webs, The (1019)
Summons to Love (1018)

Te Deum in F (0082)
These to the Front (0398)
Three Choruses (1148)
Three Irish Folk Songs (1149)
Three Partsongs (0403, 1150)
Thy Beaming Eyes (0943)

Two Folk Songs (1245)
Two Songs from the
 Thirteenth Century (0946)

Vier Lieder für Männerchor
 (0291)
Viking's Last Voyage, The
 (0409)
Voice from the Sea, A (0947)
Voyage of Columbus, The
 (0292)

Walrus and the Carpenter,
 The (0794)
War Song (0948)
Warrior's Death, The (0294)
Water Lily, The (0795)
When Love Was Young (0413)
When the Last Sea is Sailed
 (0091)
Witch, The (0952)

INDEX B: SACRED WORKS

Lobe den Herrn (0689)
Lord Dismiss Us with Thy Blessing (1092)
Lord God Omnipotent, The (0540)
Lord God, Thy Sea is Mighty (0864)
Lord Is in His Holy Temple, The (0969)
Lord Is King, The (0235)
Lord Is My Light, The (1093)
Lord Is My Shepherd, The (0047, 1186)
Lord Is My Strength and Song, The (0751)
Lord of All Beings (0048)
Lord of All Did Reign, The (0478)
Lord of All Power and Might (0351)
Lord of the Harvest (0865)
Lord of the Worlds Above (0049, 0479)
Lord Reigneth, The (0620)
Lord, Thou Hast Searched Me (1237)
Lord, What Is Man? (0621)
Lord Will Reign, The (0480)
Lord, with a Glowing Heart I'd Praise Thee (0622)
Lord's Prayer, The (0970)

Magnificat (0050, 0485, 0486, 0624, 0625, 0753, 1096, 1097, 1269)
Mary's Lullaby (0357)
Mass in C (0132)
Mass in C Minor (1238, 1271, 1272)
Mass in D (1004)
Mass in E-flat (0051, 0541)
Mass in F Minor (1273)
May the Words of My Mouth (0488)
Midnight Service for New Year's Eve (0237)
Morn's Roseate Hues (0362)
Morning Service (0133, 0134, 0194, 0238, 0239, 0240,

1098, 1239)
Moses in Egypt (0542)
Motette: Psalm 74 (0113)
Mount Carmel (0491)
Music for the Synagogue (0493)
My Heart Is Fixed, O God (1240)
My Strength Is in the Lord (0494)

Nativity, The (1006)
New River, The (0869)
Night Song of Bethlehem, The (0241)
No One Is Like Our God (0496)
Noël (0365)
Now From the Sixth Hour there Was Darkness (0242)
Nunc dimittis (0055, 0486, 0634, 0753, 1097, 1107, 1108)

O Beautiful Easter Morn (0136)
O Bless the Lord My Soul (1007)
O Cease, My Wandering Soul (0366)
O Clap Your Hands All Ye People (0244)
O Day of Rest (0367)
O God Be Merciful (0368)
O Haupt voll Blut (0690)
O Holy Child of Bethlehem (0369)
O How Amiable (0245)
O Jesus, Thou Art Standing (0636)
O Lord God of Israel (0057)
O Lord God, the Life of Mortals (0497)
O Lord, I Will Exalt Thee (1109)
O Lord Our God Arise (0058)
O Lord, Rebuke Me Not (0246)
O Lord the Proud Are Risen

INDEX C: SECULAR WORKS

March of the Monks of Bangor
   (1270)
Margarita (0356)
Masses, The (0867)
May Carol, A (0358)
May Day (0754)
May Eve (0052)
Meadowrue, The (0487)
Mein Vaterland (0112, 0236)
Merlin and Vivian (0755)
Merry Christmas (0626)
Mexican Serenade (0369)
Midnight (1274)
Midsummer Clouds (0931)
Miller's Daughter, The (0489)
Minstrel's Adieu, The (0818)
Minstrel's Catch, The (0819)
Minstrel's Song (1005)
Minstrelsy of Nature in the
   Wilds of North America
   (0820)
Miranda (0627)
Mirtil in Arcadia (0756)
Miss Nancy's Gown (0360)
Mister Moon (0361)
Moon Boat,The (0054)
Morning Song (0628)
Mortal Life Is Full of Battle
   (0490)
Morven and the Grail (1099)
Mountain   Shepherd's   Song
   (1100)
Munster Fusiliers, The (0492)
Music: An Ode (0757)
Music of the Spheres, The
   (0419)
Music, The Harmonizer of the
   World (0821)
Music   to Aristophanes Ar-
   charnians (0420)
Musical Trust, The (0758)
Musings of the Wild Wood
   (0822)
My Love (1101)
My Native Land (0971)
My Shadow (0759)
My Sweetheart Gave (0363)

National Hymn (0629, 1102)

'Neath the Elm Trees (0868)
New Earth, The (0762)
New   Hail Columbia,   The
   (0364)
New River, The (0869)
Niagara (0135, 0823)
Night (0763)
Night Has a Thousand Eyes,
   The (0495, 1103)
Nightingale and the Rose,
   The (0764)
Nights, The (0630)
No! No! It Is Not Dying
   (0632)
No! Not Despairingly (0633)
Nomanenzug (1105)
Norsemen's Raid, The (1104)
Now Sinks the Sun (1106)
Nun of Nidaros, The (0243)

O Lady Mine (0765)
O Maiden Fair (0870)
O Many and Many a Year Ago
   (0638)
O 'Twas a Joyful Sound
   (1110)
O Wise Old Alma mater (0933)
Oben wo die Sterne glühen
   (0934)
Ode (0543, 0972, 0973)
Ode by Collins (0826)
Ode to Music (0766)
Ode by Collins (0826)
Ode for Commencement Day at
   Yale (1111)
Ode for the Dedication of
   the Albright Art Gallery
   (1112)
Ode for the Opening of the
   Chicago World's Fair
   (0371)
Ode to the Sun, An (0640)
Ode Written for G.S., No. 20
   (0137)
Oedipus Tyrannus of
   Sophocles (1008)
Oh Captain! My Captain!
   (0635)
Oh Come to Me (0992)

INDEX D: TITLES OF WORKS

Festival Hymn (0194)
Festival Jubilate (0030)
Fill Your Goblets (0809, 0812)
Fireside Harmony (0989)
Fischerknabe, Der (0921)
Fisher, The (1050)
Five Four-Part Songs (0198)
Five Partsongs (1051)
Five Settings of the Venite, exultemus Domine (1228)
Five Three-Part Songs (0199)
Flag, The (0721)
Florens (1214)
Flower Songs (0447)
Flower Queen, The (1215)
For Freedom, Honor, and Native Land (0962)
For One Who Fell in Battle (0900)
For You and Me! (0851)
Fountain, The (0586, 0722)
Four Canticles (0031)
Four Choral Responses (0032)
Four Choruses (1052)
Four Partsongs (0723, 1053)
Four Songs (0448)
Four Songs of Brittany (0329)
Free Lances (1260)
Freedom Our Queen (0999, 1054)
From the Sea (0923)
Funeral Anthem (0813, 0814)
Funeral Hymn for a Soldier (1000)
Future, The (0587)

Garden Lily and the Meadow Flowers, The (0417)
Gateway of Ispahan (0449)
Gay and Sad (1180)
General Booth (0852)
Gettysburg Address (0724)
Give Ear, O Shepherd of Israel (1229)
Give Thanks to God, He Reigns on High (0990)
Give Unto the Lord (1055)
Give Unto the Lord, O Ye Mighty (0201)
Gloria in excelsis (0202, 0203, 0204, 0205, 0588, 0589, 0963)
Gloriosa patria (1056)
God of Abraham Praise, The (0207)
God Bless Our Native Land (0964)
God Is My Strong Salvation (0590)
God Is Our Refuge (0206, 0450, 0591)
God of My Life (0854)
God That Made Earth and Heaven (0592, 1057)
God To Whom We Look Up Blindly (0330)
God Who Madest Earth and Heaven (0209, 0331)
Golden Legend, The (0725)
Golden Prince, The (0725)
Golden Stars Are Quiring in the West (1058)
Gondolier's Serenade (0991)
Good Morrow (1262)
Good Night! (0212, 0726)
Gospel Call, The (0109)
Gracious Is the Lord (1230)
Grant, We Beseech Thee (1059)
Grasshopper and the Ant, The (0213)
Gray Twilight (0451)
Great Republic, The (0128, 0815)
Greek Festival Hymn (1060)
Green of Spring, The (0452)
Greenwood, The (0033)
Gute Nacht (0214)
Gypsies (0727)

Hail Beauteous Spring (0816)
Hail Us Doctors of Song (0322)
Hallelujah Chorus (0537)
Hark! Hark! My Soul (0215)
Hark! the Trumpet Calleth (0216)

APPENDIX E: AUTHORS AND TRANSLATORS

Harding, Katherine Washburn, 0763
Harte, Bret, 0505
Hartsough, Palmer, 1223
Hauergal, Francis Ridley, 0639, 1062
Hawley, Helen, 0452
Hayden, Mabel, 0769
Hayes, John Lord, 0374, 0389, 0529
Hazard, Caroline, 0491
Heber, Reginald, 0592, 0841, 1035
Heine, Heinrich, 0795, 0920, 1155, 1193
Heinrich, Anthony Phillip, 0828, 0835
Hellman, George C., 0335
Hemans, Felecia Dorothea Browne, 0375, 0619
Hemans, Francis, 0640
Hempel, Charles J., 0797
Henley, W. E., 0697
Herrick, Robert, 0524, 0562, 0563, 0701
Hewitt, Mary E., 0803
Higginson, Ella, 1150
Hildreth, Charles L., 1274
Hiles, Patricia Louise, 0083
Holmes, D. H., 1115
Holmes, Oliver Wendell, 0015, 0037, 0999, 1126, 1156
Hood, Thomas, 0769
Hooker, Brian, 1020, 1099
Hopkins, Josiah, 0890
Hovey, Richard, 0941
How, H. H., 0636
Howe, M. A. de Wolfe, 0398
Hughes, Agnes Lockhart, 0466, 0451
Hunt, Leigh, 0269
Hyatt, Alfred H., 0311, 0321
Hymnal, The, 0362
Hymns Ancient and Modern, 0151, 0189, 0215

Ingham, John Hale, 0346
Insulanus, Alanus, 0529
Irving, Washington, 0232, 0292
Ives, Charles, 0849, 0851, 0857, 0866, 0869, 0886, 0888

Jansen, Erich, 0042
Jansson, A. L., 0754
Jennings, Alice C., 1130
Johnson, Burgess, 0199
Jones, Thomas S., Jr., 0052
Judah, Daniel Ben, 0499
Julian, John, 0585

Keats, John, 0662, 0685, 1012
Keble, John, 0395
Kelley, Thomas, 1121
Kempis, Thomas à, 1021
Keppler, E., 0911
Kipling, Rudyard, 0502, 0646, 0776
Koren, John, 0382

Lang, Andrew, 0448
Langdon, William Chauncey, 0344
Langenschwartz, Dr. 0802
Lanier, Sidney, 0169, 0587, 0627, 0649
Larcom, L., 1134
Lear, Edward, 0448
Leonard, Harriet E., 0980
Lewis, Joel, 0721
Liebe, L., 0294
Lincoln, Abraham, 0724
Lind, W. Murdoch, 0364
Lindsay, N. Vachel, 0852
Lingg, Herman von, 1105
Lintott, Phyllis, 0729
Locke, C. H., 0818
Lockhart, Agnes, 0061, 0062
Long, John Luther, 1136
Longfellow, Henry W., 0230, 0243, 0255, 0262, 0445, 0463, 0512, 0534, 0884, 1068, 1088, 1134, 1193, 1261, 1280
Low, Benjamin R. C., 0860

APPENDIX F: INDEX TO THE BIBLIOGRAPHY

APPENDIX

APPENDIX: LIST OF PUBLISHERS

A-R Editions; Madison,
   Wisconsin
American Music Company
Arrow Music Press
Associated Music Publishers;
   New York

Bacon and Hart
Belwin, Inc.
Biglow and Main
Birchard, C. C.
Birchard, Summy
Boner, William H.
Boonin, Joseph, Inc.; New
   Jersey
Boosey and Hawkes; New York
Boston Conservatory Music
   Store
Boston Music Company
Bradlee, C.; Boston
Brainard's Sons, C.;
   Cleveland
Breitkopf and Härtel; Leipzig
Broadman Press

Case, Lockwood, and Brainard
   Co.
Christman, C. G.
Church, J., and Sons;
   Cincinnati
Clare
Curwen, J., and Sons

Da Capo Music Press; New York
Ditson, Oliver P., and
   Company; Boston

Empire Music Publishers
Edition Salabert; Paris and
   New York
Elliott, Charles S., and
   Company; New York

Fischer, Carl; New York
Fischer, J., and Brothers
Flammer, Harold; Delaware
   Water Gap, Penn.

Galaxy Music; New York
Gaupner; Boston
Geibel and Lehman;
   Philadelphia
Ginn and Company
Gramer and Company
Grand Conservatory
   Publishing; New York
Gray, H. W.

Harvard Univeristy Press;
   Cambridge, Mass.
Hill-Coleman
Hill and Range Songs, Inc.
Hines, Hayden, and Eldridge
Holt C., Jr.

Jenks and Palmer; Boston
Jung, P. L.; New York

Kidder, A. B.

Leidt, M., and Company; New
   York

Lorenz, E. S.
Lyon and Healy; Chicago
Martin amd Morris; Chicago
Mason and Law
Mason Brothers
Mercury Music
Merion Music
Molineaux, G.

Novello; London

Parsons, G.
Peer International; New York
Pond, William A.
Presser, Theodore; Bryn Mawr,
    Penn.

Ricordi, G.; New York
Root and Cady
Row, R.D., and Company
Russell Brothers; Boston
Russell, G. D.

Saalfield
Sängerfest; Boston
Schirmer, G.; New York
Schmidt, Arthur P., and
    Company; Leipzig and
    Boston

Scribner Sons, Charles'; New
    York
Shelpley and Wright
Silver Burdett
Southern Music; San Antonio,
    Texas

Tappan, Whittemore, and
    Mason
Thiebes-Stierlin; St. Louis
Thompson, C. W.; Boston
Tolman, Henry, and Company;
    Boston
Tourjée; Boston

Ward and Company
White, Smith, and Company;
    Boston
Wilkins, J. H., and Carter,
    R. B.; Boston
Wood, B. F.
Wright Printers, A. J.; 3
Water St., Boston

Yale University Press; New
    Haven, Conn.